Martin Luther—

Martin Luther—
Reformer
or Revolutionary?

Random House 

Third Edition

987654321

Copyright © 1967, 1972, 1976,
1977 by Random House, Inc.

Library of Congress Cataloging in Publication Data
Main entry under title:
Martin Luther—Reformer or Revolutionary?
  (Random House Historical Pamphlet Edition; 7)
  Reprint of a section of the 3rd ed. of Great Issues in
Western Civilization edited by B. Tierney, D. Kagan, and
L. P. Williams.
    1. Luther, Martin; 1483-1546—Addresses, essays, lectures.
I. Series: Great Issues in Western Civilization; 7.
CB245.G68 1977 no. 7 [BR326] 909'.09'821s
ISBN 0-394-32055-7 [230'.4'10924] 76-48950

Acknowledgments

(Page numbers for articles in this text appear before each acknowledgment.)

P. 6   Jacob Whimpheling, "Response," from Gerald Strauss, *Manifestations of Discontent in Germany on the Eve of the Reformation* (1971), pp. 41–45. Reprinted by permission of Indiana University Press.

P. 9/P. 42   Gordon Rupp, *The Righteousness of God: Luther Studies* (1953), pp. 3–15/pp. 121–127. Reprinted by permission of Hodder & Stoughton Ltd., London.

P. 14   "Martin Luther's Letter to George Spalatin," from *Luther's Correspondence and Other Contemporary Letters*, trans. by P. Smith (1913), Vol. 1, pp. 28–29, 33–35, 98. Reprinted by permission of Fortress Press.

P. 15   "Martin Luther's Letter to George Spenlein," from *Luther's Correspondence and Other Contemporary Letters,* Vol. 1, pp. 33–35.

P. 16   Martin Luther, "Disputation Against Scholastic Theology," from *Luther's Works*, Helmut T. Lehman and Jaroslav Pelikan eds., (1957), Vol. 31, pp. 9–12. Reprinted by permission of Fortress Press.

P. 19   Martin Luther, "Ninety-five Theses," from *Luther's Works*, Vol. 31, pp. 25–29.

P. 21   "Maximilian's Letter to Leo X," from *Luther's Correspondence and Other Contemporary Letters*, Vol. 1, p. 98. (Fortress Press)

P. 22   Martin Luther, "Address to the Christian Nobility of the German Nation," from *Three Treatises* (1947), pp. 10–16, 20–25. Reprinted by permission of Fortress Press.

P. 28   ———,"A Treatise on Christian Liberty," from *Three Treatises*, pp. 251–255.

P. 31   Martin Luther, "Speech Before Emperor Charles," from *Luther's Works*, Vol. 32, pp. 109–112. (Fortress Press)

P. 35   Erik H. Erikson, *Young Man Luther* (1958), pp. 14–16, 20–21, 206–213. Reprinted from *Young Man Luther* by Erik H. Erikson. By permission of W. W. Norton & Company, Inc. Copyright © 1958, 1962 by Erik H. Erikson.

P. 47   From *The Protestant Reformation* by Henri Daniel-Rops, pp. 9–26, translated by Audrey Butler. Translation copyright © 1961 by E. P. Dutton & Co., Inc., and reprinted with their permission.

Preface

A major purpose of this series of pamphlets is to convince students in Western civilization courses that the essential task of a historian is not to collect dead facts but to confront live issues. The issues are alive because they arise out of the tensions that men have to face in every generation—tensions between freedom and authority, between reason and faith, between human free will and all the impersonal circumstances that help to shape our lives.

In order to achieve any sophisticated understanding of such matters, students need to read the views of great modern historians as they are set out in their own words. Students need to develop a measure of critical historical insight by comparing these often conflicting views with the source material on which they are based. They need above all to concern themselves with the great issues that have shaped the course of Western civilization and not with historical "problems" that are mere artificially contrived conundrums.

We believe that there are three major themes whose development and interplay have shaped the distinctive characteristics that set Western civilization apart from the other great historic cultures. They are the growth of a tradition of rational scientific inquiry, the persistence of a tension between Judaeo-Christian religious ideals and social realities, and the emergence of constitutional forms of government. These three themes are introduced in the first pamphlets of the series. Readers will find them recurring in new forms and changing contexts throughout the rest of the pamphlets. We hope that in studying them they will come to a richer understanding of the heritage of Western civilization—and of the historian's approach to it.

BRIAN TIERNEY
DONALD KAGAN
L. PEARCE WILLIAMS

Martin Luther—

CONTENTS

QUESTIONS FOR STUDY

1 *What was Luther's position on the relation of God to man?*

2 *To what extent was Luther heretical before the indulgence controversy?*

3 *What, according to Luther, was the true liberty of a Christian?*

4 *What role in the making of the Reformation do the various historians cited assign to Luther?*

5 *Would there have been a Reformation if Luther had never lived?*

The advent of the Protestant Reformation is generally taken to mark the end of the Middle Ages in northern Europe and the beginnings of the modern world. The unity of Western Christendom was destroyed and one of the most important medieval ideals—that of the unified, Christian, Catholic empire—was dealt a death blow. In its place emerged the idea of the nation-state in which, ultimately, the religion of the state became a question of national policy. The sixteenth-century formula cujus regio, ejus religio ("the religion of the ruler shall be the religion of the ruled") explicitly acknowledged the breakdown of the monopoly of religious truth and practice exercised by the Catholic Church for more than a millennium. From this breakdown was to emerge the emphasis upon individual conscience, religious tolerance, and awareness of cultural and national differences that marks the modern world.

The Reformation was a revolution of considerable magnitude. Moreover, all the aforementioned modern elements, except tolerance, were present in the "pre-revolutionary" times. Martin Luther's individual conscience was what drove him into religious orders and ultimately into religious rebellion. Luther was intensely German in his outlook and was quite aware of the cultural gulf between Germany and Latin Christendom. The national question was also present in the Germany of the early sixteenth century. German gold flowed to Rome, and the Germans resented it. The policies and politics of Rome influenced the German scene, and some of the German princes resented this too. Finally, the ideal of Christian unity, which was to appeal so strongly to Charles V, elected Holy Roman Emperor in 1519, was a threat to the independence of these princes, and it has been argued that they protected Luther and embraced Protestantism less because of sincere religious belief than because of *political expediency. All of this has led some historians to see the Protestant Reformation as both inevitable and impersonal. The Reformation, they argue, was the inevitable result of the economic, social, and political development of Germany in the fifteenth century. If it had not been initiated by Luther, it would have been started by someone else. Luther just happened to be the one who threw down the challenge to the church.*

It is, of course, impossible to answer the question "Would the Reformation have occurred if Luther had never lived?" since Luther did live and there is no way to alter that. We can, however, question the answer given by those who would make Luther a mere cipher in the coming of the Reformation. After all, the church had been corrupt in previous ages and had been successfully reformed. Other times had witnessed resentment of Rome and princes jealous of their powers without also undergoing irreparable schism. Might not the difference between these times and the early sixteenth century be precisely the presence of one man, Luther? This is not to say that Luther, single-handedly, made the Reformation. But it is to suggest that there were essential ingredients in the Reformation that owed their existence to his personal and unique experiences. Not the least of these ingredients was Luther's determination to purify the faith. We can legitimately ask a number of questions about this aspect of the Reformation, and we may also expect to find historical evidence to permit us to draw some rather firm conclusions from it. For example, did Luther's initial hostility to Rome derive from any of the aforementioned social, economic, and political "sources" of the Reformation, or were they much more personal? Did the selling of indulgences trigger Luther's attack on corruption in Rome, or was this merely the occasion for Luther to launch a much more fundamental attack against theoretical theology rather than corrupt practice? Finally, did Luther really be-

lieve that he could reform the church? Certainly all the public issues were negotiable. What was not was Luther's private conviction that he had found the way to salvation and that this way, to put it mildly, appeared to conflict with the traditional way of the Catholic Church. It was this private conviction that sustained Luther in the years of battle that were to ensue. As historians we may legitimately ask its source from the historical evidence, and if we discover it, we may then attempt to understand how such a private conviction could receive such widespread public support.

The problem posed by the documents that follow is central to all historical investigation. It involves the question of the role of the individual in historical crises and, as a subsidiary issue, the question of whether an individual actually knows what he is doing. For even if we accept the thesis that Luther, the man, was essential to the Reformation, we must still ask to what extent Luther was merely the vehicle for the expression of more general social or psychological forces. The reader should be aware of the fact that no answer can be proved but that some answer must be given. How he decides will affect his interpretation of the past and his actions in the present.

1 *The Road to Reformation*

In May 1515 Jacob Wimpheling wrote a "response" to a famous letter on Germany written by Enea Silvio Piccolomini (later Pius II) in 1457 in which he detailed the grievances of the Germans against papal misrule. This is what the church looked like to a devout member just two years before Luther posted his famous theses.

FROM *Response* BY *Jacob Wimpheling*

RIGHTLY DOES ENEA SILVIO PRAISE Germany as the source of his elevation [to cardinal]. Because he is an Italian, however, and loves the land of his birth, he would not enjoy seeing the flow of money from our country to his own slowed to a trickle. He therefore flatters us with stories of the translation of the *imperium* from the Greeks to the Germans, though we all know that our ancestors had to win this imperium with their courage and their life's blood. He goes on to laud the ample treasures to be found in our churches and homes. But even if Germany really did possess so abundant a store of hard-earned and frugally managed wealth, how much of it would remain to us after we had taken care of our daily needs, had seen to the maintenance of our churches, cities, streets, and public institutions, assured our country's protection from its enemies, provided for orphans, widows, and the victims of plague, pox, and French disease, and comforted beggars, as Christian piety demands?

Enea makes much of the fact that we Germans received our Christian faith from his compatriots. "Rome," he writes, "preached Christ to you; it was faith in Christ, received from Rome, that extinguished barbarism in you." We concede, of course, that missionaries from Rome brought the saving message of Christ to our land. But by the same token Rome herself was, like Germany, converted to the Christian faith, and Rome should therefore show no less gratitude than Germany for the reception of her faith. For was it not Peter, a Jew from Palestine, who preached the Gospel of Christ in Rome? If Enea's argument were applied to the Romans themselves, they would now be obliged to send annual tributes of gold and silver to Syria. . . .

It is not that we deny our debt to Rome. But we ask: Is Rome not also indebted to us? Have not two of our compatriots, clever and skillful men hailing from Strassburg and Mainz, invented the noble art of printing, which makes it possible to propagate the correct doctrines of faith and morals throughout the world and in all languages? . . . Do we, who have been true and industrious in our service to religion and to the Holy Roman Church, who are steadfast in our faith and even—as Enea admits—prepared to shed our blood for it, who willingly obey orders, buy indulgences, travel to Rome, and send money—do we who perform all these duties deserve to be called barbarians? . . . Despite this slanderous label, Enea speaks with lavish praise of our fatherland, of our cities and buildings. For what purpose? For one only: to make our ears more receptive to the demands coming from Rome dressed in Christian garb but serving Italian interests; in other words, to put us in the mood for wasting our fortunes on foreigners. . . . As it is, our compatriots crowd the road to Rome. They pay for papal reservations and dispensations. They appear before papal courts—and not always because they have appealed a case to Rome, but rather because their cases have been arbitrarily transferred there. Is there a nation more patient and willing to receive indulgences, though we well know that the income from them is divided between the Holy See and its officialdom? Have we not paid dearly for the confirmation of every bishop and abbot? . . .

Thus we are done out of fortune, and for no purpose other than to support the innumerable retainers and hangers-on that populate the papal court. Enea himself gives us a list of these papal lackeys, the number of which increases daily. True, if the pope must furnish court rooms for all the legal business in Christendom, he requires a huge staff. But there is no need for this. Apart from imperial courts, there exist in our German cities learned and honorable judges to whom appeals from lower episcopal courts could be directed. It is in the highest degree objectionable that Rome bypasses courts of higher resort—often on trivial pretexts or out of pique—and compels our compatriots, laymen included, to appear in Rome. No one will deny that intricate and weighty matters should be appealed to Rome as the seat of highest power and of greatest wisdom and justice. But the rights of imperial and episcopal jurisdiction must not be infringed. If these rights had remained intact, the Apostolic See would not today stagger under an unmanageable weight of legal and administrative business. . . .

The Council of Basel pointed out that our sacred church fathers had written their canons for the purpose of assuring the Church of good government, and that honor, discipline, faith, piety, love, and peace reigned in the Church as long as these regulations were observed. Later, however, vanity and greed began to prevail; the laws of the fathers were neglected, and the Church sank into immorality and depravity, debasement, degradation and abuse of office. This is principally due to papal reservations of prelacies and other ecclesiastical benefices, also to the prolific award of expectancies to future benefices, and to innumerable concessions and other burdens placed upon churches and clergy. To wit:

Church incomes and benefices are given to unworthy men and Italians.

High offices and lucrative posts are awarded to persons of unproven merit and character.

Few holders of benefices reside in their churches, for as they hold several posts simultaneously they cannot reside in all of them at once. Most do not even recognize the faces of their parishioners. They neglect the care of souls and seek only temporal rewards.

The divine service is curtailed.

Hospitality is diminished.

Church laws lose their force.

Ecclesiastical buildings fall into ruin.

The conduct of clerics is an open scandal.

Able, learned, and virtuous priests who might raise the moral and professional level of the clergy abandon their studies because they see no prospect of advancement.

The ranks of the clergy are riven by rivalry and animosity; hatred, envy, and even the wish for the death of others are aroused.

Striving after pluralities of benefices is encouraged.

Poor clerics are maltreated, impoverished, and forced from their posts.

Crooked lawsuits are employed to gather benefices.

Some benefices are procured through simony.

Other benefices remain vacant.

Able young men are left to lead idle and vagrant lives.

Prelates are deprived of jurisdiction and authority.

The hierarchical order of the Church is destroyed.

In this manner, a vast number of violations of divine and human law is committed and condoned. . . . "It is the pope's special mission," writes Enea, "to protect Christ's sheep. He should accomplish this task in such a way as to lead all men to the path of salvation. He must see that the pure Gospel is preached to all, that false doctrines, blasphemies, and unchristian teachings are eradicated, and that enemies of the faith are driven from the lands of Christendom. He must heal schisms and end wars, abolish robbery, murder, arson, adultery, drunkenness and gluttony, spite, hatred and strife. He must promote peace and order, so that concord might reign among men, and honor and praise be given to God."

So Enea. My question is: Does a court of ephebes and muleteers and flatterers help the pope prevent schism and abolish blasphemy, wars, robbery, and the other crimes mentioned by Enea? Would he not be better served by men learned in canon law and Scripture, by men who know how to preach and can help the faithful ease their conscience in the confessional? The Council of Basel was surely inspired when it decreed that a third of all benefices should go to men versed in the Bible. . . . If I am not mistaken, the conciliar fathers wished to see the true Gospel of Christ preached everywhere. They wished honor and glory given to God. We ourselves want nothing else. We would rejoice if many men were to praise God, if every priest in his sufficiently endowed benefice were to serve God and celebrate the Eucharist, if popes and emperors, if the whole Church were to draw rich benefit from this holy work, the most efficacious office of them all. . . .

The English historian Gordon Rupp puts Luther and the problems facing him at the very outset of the Reformation in historical perspective.

FROM *The Righteousness of God* BY *Gordon Rupp*

IT WAS A CRITICAL MOMENT during the Leipzig Disputation (1519) when Martin Luther, out-manoeuvred by his opponent, Dr. Eck, was goaded into declaring that "among the articles of John Huss . . . which were condemned, are many which are truly Christian." The audience was horrified, and perhaps Luther himself was a little shocked. For he had grown to accept the judgment of contemporary opinion against the heretic of a former generation. "I used to abhor the very name of Huss. So zealous was I for the Pope that I would have helped to bring iron and fire to kill Huss, if not in very deed, at least with a consenting mind." In this verdict faith and party loyalty combined, for the Erfurt Augustinians were proud that a member of their own order, John Zachariae, had earned the title "Scourge of Huss" and his tomb bore in effigy the Golden Rose bestowed upon him by a grateful Pope. It was not until Luther himself entered a similar context of Papal condemnation that he turned to examine the writings of Huss, and to criticize this unexamined assumption. Then indeed he could cry to Spalatin, "We are all Hussites, without knowing it . . . even Paul and Augustine!"

*   *   *

Luther prided himself on the fact that while others had attacked the manners and the morals of particular popes, or the abuses and corruptions of the Curia, he had begun with doctrine. We know that in its essentials Luther's theology existed before the opening of the Church struggle in 1517, and that it was not an improvization devised in the course of that conflict. Nevertheless, it was as the conflict developed out of the Indulgence controversy that he began to question the basis of the Papal power, and turned to the issues raised in a preceding generation by the theologians of the Conciliar movement, the question whether the Papacy were of divine or of human institution. Early in 1519 he could still write, "If unfortunately there are such things in Rome as might be improved, there neither is, nor can be, any reason that one should tear oneself away from the Church in schism. Rather, the worse things become, the more a man should help, and cling to her, for by schism and contempt nothing can be mended." In fateful weeks before the Leipzig Disputation, Luther studied church history and the Papal decretals. On 13th March 1519 he wrote to his friend Spalatin, "I do not know whether the Pope is Anti-Christ himself, or only his apostle, so grievously is Christ, i.e. Truth, manhandled and crucified by him in these decretals."

The Leipzig Disputation forced Luther to face the implications of his revolt, and made him realize that he could not come so far, without going further in repudiation of papal authority. Then, early in 1520, he read Hutten's edition of Valla's exposure of the "Donation of Constantine," and he wrote in disgust, "I have hardly any doubt left that the Pope is the very Anti-Christ himself, whom the common report expects, so well do all the things he lives, does, speaks, ordains, fit the picture."

In June 1520 he wrote solemn, final words, in a writing of exceptional vehemence. "Farewell, unhappy, hopeless, blasphemous Rome! The wrath of God is come upon thee, as thou deservest. . . . We have cared for Babylon, and she is not healed: let us leave her then, that she may be the habitation of dragons, spectres and witches, and true to her name of Babel, an everlasting confusion, a new pantheon of wickedness."

There are battles of the mind which most men cannot go on fighting again and again. We make up our minds, as we say, and the account is settled. Thereafter we reopen that particular issue only with great reluctance. No doubt this is a weakness of our spirit, though to be able to keep an open mind requires detachment from the hurly-burly of decision, and is more easily achieved in academic groves than in the battlefield or marketplace or temple. Luther's words here perhaps show us the point at which he hardened his mind with terrible finality against the Papacy, as later on he reached a point at which Zwingli and Erasmus were to him as heathen men and publicans. He had become convinced that the Papacy had become the tool of the Devil, that it was blasphemous . . . "possessed and oppressed by Satan, the damned seat of Anti-Christ."

The papacy which Luther attacked was not the Post-Tridentine papacy. On the other hand, he meant something more when he called it "Anti-Christ" than we mean by the adjective "Anti-Christian." Like many great Christians from St. Cyprian to Lord Shaftesbury, Luther believed himself to be living in the last age of the world, on the very edge of time. He believed that the papacy was toppling to its doom, and that this fate was a merited judgment upon a perversion of spiritual power to which there could be no parallel in the temporal realm, and for which only one category would serve, the Biblical category of Anti-Christ.

There are striking words in his "Of Good Works" (1520) which go to the root of this conviction. "There is not such great danger in the temporal power as in the spiritual, when it does wrong. For the temporal power can do no harm, since it has nothing to do with preaching and faith, and the first three commandments. But the spiritual power does harm not only when it does wrong, but also when it neglects its duty and busies itself with other things, even if they were better than the very best works of the temporal power." For Luther the blessed thing for men and institutions is that they should be where God intends them, doing what God has called them to do, and the cursed thing for men and institutions is when they run amok in God's ordered creation, going where God has not sent them, and occupied with other things than their divine vocation.

The papacy had become entangled in diplomatic, juridical, political, financial pressure. Its crime was not that these things were necessarily bad in themselves, but that for their sake the awful, supreme, God-given task of the pastoral care and the cure of souls had been neglected and forsaken. Two consequences had followed. In the first place, it had become a tyranny, like any other institution which succumbs before the temptation of power. In that exposition of the Magnificat, which was interrupted by the famous journey to Worms in 1521, Luther had profoundly diagnosed this corrupting effect of power upon institutions. The tract embodies Luther's reflections upon the fate of great Empires in the Bible and in secular history. It is not empire, but the abuse of it which is wrong. "For while the earth remains authority, rule, power . . . must needs remain. But God will not suffer men to abuse them. He puts down one kingdom, and exalts another: increases one people and destroys another: as he did with Assyria, Babylon, Persia, Greece and Rome, though they thought they should sit in their seats forever."

But when empire is abused, then power becomes an incentive to arrogance, and a terrible inflation begins. These institutions or individuals swell and stretch their authority with a curious bubble-like, balloon-like quality. Outwardly they seem omnipotent, and those who take them at their face value can be paralysed and brought into bondage to them. But in fact they are hollow shams, corroded from within, so that doom comes upon them, that swift collapse so often the fate of tyrants and empires. "When their bubble is full blown, and everyone supposes them to have won and overcome, and they feel themselves safe and secure, then God pricks the bubble . . . and it is all over . . . therefore their prosperity has its day, disappears like a bubble, and is as if it had never been." It is interesting that Shakespeare turns to the same metaphor when he describes the fall of Wolsey:

> I have ventured,
> Like little wanton boys that swim on bladders,
> This many summers in a sea of glory,
> But far beyond my depth: my high-blown pride
> At length broke under me.

Luther is fond of punning on the double meaning of the Latin word "Bulla," which means bubble, but also the papal bull.

It may well be that Luther's meditation on this quality of tyranny derives from his own experiences, 1517–20. The initial threat of excommunication, and the final promulgation of the papal bull had a deep significance for him. These were the challenge which focussed all his doubts and fears, and evoked his courage at a time when he had no reason to anticipate anything but the dire fate prophesied for him by friends and foes. But, in fact, these papal sanctions led to the revelation of the weakness of the papal authority, a revelation of immense significance, from which all over Christendom (not forgetting the England of Henry VIII) men could draw their own conclusions. It was not that a man could defy the papacy and get away with it. After all, Wyclif had died in his bed, and throughout most of the Middle Ages there were parts of Europe where heresy flourished openly. But there was a new background which echoed and reverberated Luther's defiance, and a concentration of public attention on it which rallied great historical forces.

For centuries the papal sanctions had been as thunder and lightning, and there had been times and places when princes and peoples had cowered before them. Even now the sonorous phrases, the hallowed ritual, did not lack of menacing effect and struck deep into Luther's mind, always hypersensitive to words. The extraordinary agitation of his sermon, "On the Power of Excommunication" (1518), an utterance so outspoken that it was perhaps more effectual than the Ninety-five Theses in securing his impeachment, reveals the tension in his mind. It is noticeable that in the printed elaboration of this sermon he turns to the "bladder" motif. "They say . . . our Ban must be feared, right or wrong. With this saying they insolently comfort themselves, swell their chests, and puff themselves up like adders, and almost dare to defy heaven, and to threaten the whole world: with this bugaboo they have made a deep and mighty impression, imagining that there is more in these words than there really is. Therefore we would explain them more fully, and prick this bladder which with its three peas makes such a frightful noise." The publication of the Bull in 1520 evoked the same tension, and in his writings against it he affirms, "The Truth is asserting itself and will burst all the bladders of the Papists."

Only gradually did Luther and his friends realize how the world had changed since the days of Huss, that the Diet of Worms would not be as the Council of Constance, though the devout Charles V might be as anxious to dispose of heretics as any Emperor Sigismund. Now the accumulated weight of the past intervened, with paralysing effect. An enormous moral prestige had been frittered away, and the papal authority was revealed as a weak thing in comparison with the deep moving tide of anti-clericalism, nationalism and the fierce energies of a changing society.

But the papacy is for Luther not simply a tyranny, which can be described, as a liberal historian might describe it, in terms of the corrupting influence of power. Its tyranny is of a unique kind, for which there can only be one category, the demonic, Biblical category of Anti-Christ. By its entanglement with law and politics, the papacy has brought the souls of men and women into bondage, has confused disastrously the Law and Gospel, has become the antithesis of the Word of God which comes to free and liberate men's souls. Thus he cannot regard the papacy simply as a corrupt institution, as did the mediaeval moralists and the heretics. In Luther's later writings the papacy is included along with the Law, Sin and Death among the tyrants who beset the Christians, and is part of a view of salvation which demands an apocalyptic interpretation of history.

Two sets of Luther's writings are of special virulence: those against the Jews, the apostates of the Old Israel, and those against the Pope, the apostate of the New. Against what he considered the capital sin of blasphemy Luther turned all his invective. It is noticeable that like Ezekiel, he turned to an imagery of physical repulsion. Blasphemy and apostasy are not simply evil: they are filthy things, which must be described in language coarse enough and repulsive enough to nauseate the reader. That is not in any sense to excuse Luther's language, or to justify his reading of the papacy. But those sadly over-simplify who see in these tracts the vapourings of a dirty mind.

Luther's epitaph was premature. He had indeed plagued the papacy. He could say, "While I slept or drank Wittenberg beer with my Philip and my Amsdorf, the Word so greatly weakened the Papacy that never Prince or Emperor inflicted such damage on it." He did not kill the papacy, but in strange partnership with Ignatius Loyola, the Popes of the Counter-Reformation, the Society of Jesus, not to mention the Anabaptists, he had provoked a new historical pattern which made an end, for good and all, of the peculiar perversions of the later Middle Ages. But I think we can understand how it seemed to him that the papacy was doomed and dying, how it seemed to him the engine of Satin, the embodiment of Anti-Christ in what he believed to be the closing act of the human drama.

*　　*　　*

2   *Luther Before the Controversy Over Indulgences*

The Reuchlin case, to which Luther alludes in this letter, is one of considerable complexity, involving the place of Hebraic studies in Christian theology. This issue need not concern us here; what is important is Luther's attitude toward both Reuchlin's approach—which he was to imitate when he proposed the Ninety-five Theses for debate in 1517—and the importance of Scripture.

Martin Luther's Letter to George Spalatin

Wittenberg (January or February, 1514).

PEACE BE WITH YOU, Reverend Spalatin! Brother John Lang has just asked me what I think of the innocent and learned John Reuchlin and his prosecutors at Cologne, and whether he is in danger of heresy. You know that I greatly esteem and like the man, and perchance my judgment will be suspected, because, as I say, I am not free and neutral; nevertheless as you wish it I will give my opinion, namely that in all his writings there appears to be absolutely nothing dangerous.

I much wonder at the men of Cologne ferreting out such an obscure perplexity, worse tangled than the Gordian knot as they say, in a case as plain as day. Reuchlin himself has often protested his innocence, and solemnly asserts he is only proposing questions for debate, not laying down articles of faith, which alone, in my opinion, absolves him, so that had he the dregs of all known heresies in his memorial, I should believe him sound and pure of faith. For if such protests and expressions of opinion are not free from danger, we must needs fear that these inquisitors, who strain at gnats though they swallow camels, should at their own pleasure pronounce the orthodox heretics, no matter how much the accused protested their innocence.

What shall I say? that they are trying to cast out Beelzebub but not by the finger of God. I often regret and deplore that we Christians have begun to be wise abroad and fools at home. A hundred times worse blasphemies than this exist in the very streets of Jerusalem, and the high places are filled with spiritual idols. We ought to show our excessive zeal in removing these offences which are our real, intestine enemies. Instead of which we abandon all that is really urgent and turn to foreign and external affairs, under the inspiration of the devil who intends that we should neglect our own business without helping that of others.

Pray can anything be imagined more foolish and imprudent than such zeal? Has unhappy Cologne no waste places nor turbulence in her own church, to which she could devote her knowledge, zeal and charity, that she must needs search out such cases as this in remote parts?

But what am I doing? My heart is fuller of these thoughts than my tongue can tell. I have come to the conclusion that the Jews will always curse and blaspheme God and his King Christ, as all the prophets have predicted. He who neither reads nor understands this, as yet knows no theology, in my opinion. And so I presume the men of Cologne cannot understand the Scripture, because it is necessary that such things take place to fulfill prophecy. If they are trying to stop the Jews blaspheming, they are working to prove the Bible and God liars.

But trust God to be true, even if a million men of Cologne sweat to make him false. Conversion of the Jews will be the work of God alone operating from within, and not of man working—or rather playing—from without. If these offences be taken away, worse will follow. For they are thus given over by the wrath of God to reprobation, that they may become incorrigible, as Ecclesiastes says, for every one who is incorrigible is rendered worse rather than better by correction.

Farewell in the Lord; pardon my words, and pray the Lord for my sinning soul.

Your brother,
MARTIN LUTHER

Spenlein was a fellow Augustinian brother to whom Luther could reveal his most intimate thoughts on theology and the relation of man to God. The date (April 8, 1516) is significant, a year and a half before Luther posted his Ninety-five Theses.

Martin Luther's Letter to George Spenlein

Wittenberg, April 8, 1516.

GRACE AND PEACE to you from God the Father and the Lord Jesus Christ.

Dear Brother George:
Now I would like to know whether your soul, tired of her own righteousness, would learn to breathe and confide in the righteousness of Christ. For in our age the temptation to presumption besets many, especially those who try to be just and good before all men, not knowing the righteousness of God, which is most bountifully and freely given us in Christ. Thus they long seek to do right by themselves, that they may have courage to stand before God as though fortified with their own virtues and merits, which is impossible. You yourself were

of this opinion, or rather error, and so was I, who still fight against the error and have not yet conquered it.

Therefore, my sweet brother, learn Christ and him crucified; learn to pray to him despairing of yourself, saying: Thou, Lord Jesus, art my righteousness, but I am thy sin; thou has taken on thyself what thou wast not, and hast given to me what I was not. Beware of aspiring to such purity that you will not wish to seem to yourself, or to be, a sinner. For Christ only dwells in sinners. For that reason he descended from heaven, where he dwelt among the righteous, that he might dwell among sinners. Consider that kindness of his, and you will see his sweetest consolation. . . .

If you firmly believe this (and he is accursed who does not believe it) then take up your untaught and erring brothers, patiently uphold them, make their sins yours, and, if you have any goodness, let it be theirs. Thus the apostle teaches: Receive one another even as Christ received you, for the glory of God, and again: Have this mind in you which was also in Christ Jesus, who, when he was in the form of God, humbled himself, &c. Thus do you, if you seem pretty good to yourself, not count it as booty, as though it were yours alone, but humble yourself, forget what you are, and be as one of them that you may carry them. . . . Do this, my brother, and the Lord be with you. Farewell in the Lord.

Your brother,
Martin Luther, Augustinian

Luther, as a professor of theology, had been thoroughly grounded in the Scholastic philosophy of the Middle Ages. Of the three pillars upon which Scholastic theology rested —Scripture, the writings of the church fathers, and the philosophy of Aristotle—Scripture had become increasingly de-emphasized by Luther's time. It was to remind people that the central point of the scriptural message was not the achievement of philosophical distinctions but the salvation of man's soul that Luther composed his disputation against Scholastic theology in 1517.

Disputation Against Scholastic Theology BY *Martin Luther*

It is therefore true that man, being a bad tree, can only will and do evil. [Cf. Matt. 7:17–18.]

It is false to state that man's inclination is free to choose between either of two opposites. Indeed, the inclination is not free, but captive. This is said in opposition to common opinion.

It is false to state that the will can by nature conform to correct precept. . . .

As a matter of fact, without the grace of God the will produces an act that is perverse and evil.

It does not, however, follow that the will is by nature evil, that is, essentially evil; as the Manichaeans maintain.

It is nevertheless innately and inevitably evil and corrupt.

*   *   *

No act is done according to nature that is not an act of concupiscence against God.

Every act of concupiscence against God is evil and a fornication of the spirit.

*   *   *

The best and infallible preparation for grace and the sole means of obtaining grace is the eternal election and predestination of God.

On the part of man, however, nothing precedes grace except ill will and even rebellion against grace.

*   *   *

In brief, man by nature has neither correct precept nor good will.

It is not true that an invincible ignorance excuses one completely (all scholastics notwithstanding);

For ignorance of God and oneself and good works is by nature always invincible.

Nature, moreover, inwardly and necessarily glories and takes pride in every work which is apparently and outwardly good.

There is no moral virtue without either pride or sorrow, that is, without sin.

We are never lords of our actions, but servants. This in opposition to the philosophers.

We do not become righteous by doing righteous deeds but, having been made righteous, we do righteous deeds. This in opposition to the philosophers.

Virtually the entire *Ethics* of Aristotle is the worst enemy of grace. This in opposition to the scholastics.

It is an error to maintain that Aristotle's statement concerning happiness does not contradict Catholic doctrine. This in opposition to the doctrine on morals.

It is an error to say that no man can become a theologian without Aristotle. This in opposition to common opinion.

Indeed, no one can become a theologian unless he becomes one without Aristotle.

To state that a theologian who is not a logician is a monstrous heretic—this is a monstrous and heretical statement. This in opposition to common opinion.

In vain does one fashion a logic of faith, a substitution brought about without regard for limit and measure. This in opposition to the new dialecticians.

No syllogistic form is valid when applied to divine terms. . . .

Nevertheless it does not for that reason follow that the truth of the doctrine of the Trinity contradicts syllogistic forms. . . .

If a syllogistic form of reasoning holds in divine matters, then the doctrine of the Trinity is demonstrable and not the object of faith.

Briefly, the whole Aristotle is to theology as darkness is to light. This in opposition to the scholastics.

3 Luther and the Break with Rome

The doctrine of indulgences had a long history before Luther posted his opposition to it on October 31, 1517. It was based on Matthew 16:18–19: "Thou art Peter, and upon this rock I will build my church; and the gates of hell shall not prevail against it. And I will give unto thee the keys of the kingdom of heaven: and whatsoever thou shalt bind on earth shall be bound in heaven: and whatsoever thou shalt loose on earth shall be loosed in heaven."

Thus Christ granted to St. Peter (and to his successors, the popes) the power to remit the penalties for sins. This power was eagerly exploited by the Renaissance popes, who found themselves in almost constant financial difficulties.

Luther's challenge to debate the doctrine of indulgences, however, was not restricted to a narrow issue. It ranged over many fundamental points of church doctrine. Did Luther really believe that such basic things could be reformed? Or, without really facing up to it, must he not have known that he was proposing nothing less than a revolution?

Ninety-five Theses BY Martin Luther

OUT OF LOVE AND zeal for truth and the desire to bring it to light, the following theses will be publicly discussed at Wittenberg under the chairmanship of the reverend father Martin Luther, Master of Arts and Sacred Theology and regularly appointed Lecturer on these subjects at that place. He requests that those who cannot be present to debate orally with us will do so by letter.

In the Name of Our Lord Jesus Christ. Amen.

When our Lord and Master Jesus Christ said, "Repent" [Matt. 4:17], he willed the entire life of believers to be one of repentance.

This word cannot be understood as referring to the sacrament of penance, that is, confession and satisfaction, as administered by the clergy.

Yet it does not mean solely inner repentance; such inner repentance is worthless unless it produces various outward mortifications of the flesh.

The penalty of sin remains as long as the hatred of self, that is, true inner repentance, until our entrance into the kingdom of heaven.

The pope neither desires nor is able to remit any penalties except those imposed by his own authority or that of the canons.

The pope cannot remit any guilt, except by declaring and showing that it has been remitted by God; or, to be sure, by remitting guilt in cases reserved to his judgment. If his right to grant remission in these cases were disregarded, the guilt would certainly remain unforgiven.

*   *   *

The dying are freed by death from all penalties, are already dead as far as the canon laws are concerned, and have a right to be released from them.

Imperfect piety or love on the part of the dying person necessarily brings with it great fear; and the smaller the love, the greater the fear.

This fear or horror is sufficient in itself, to say nothing of other things, to constitute the penalty of purgatory, since it is very near the horror of despair.

Hell, purgatory, and heaven seem to differ the same as despair, fear, and assurance of salvation.

*   *   *

If remission of all penalties whatsoever could be granted to anyone at all, certainly it would be granted only to the most perfect, that is, to very few.

For this reason most people are necessarily deceived by that indiscriminate and high-sounding promise of release from penalty.

*   *   *

The pope does very well when he grants remission to souls in purgatory, not by the power of the keys, which he does not have, but by way of intercession for them.

They preach only human doctrines who say that as soon as the money clinks into the money chest, the soul flies out of purgatory.

It is certain that when money clinks in the money chest, greed and avarice can be increased; but when the church intercedes, the result is in the hands of God alone.

*   *   *

Any truly repentant Christian has a right to full remission of penalty and guilt, even without indulgence letters.

Any true Christian, whether living or dead, participates in all the blessings of Christ and the church; and this is granted him by God, even without indulgence letters.

*   *   *

If, therefore, indulgences were preached according to the spirit and intention of the pope, all these doubts would be readily resolved. Indeed, they would not exist.

Away then with all those prophets who say to the people of Christ, "Peace, peace," and there is no peace! [Jer. 6:14.]

Blessed be all those prophets who say to the people of Christ, "Cross, cross," and there is no cross!

Christians should be exhorted to be diligent in following Christ, their head, through penalties, death, and hell;

And thus be confident of entering into heaven through many tribulations rather than through the false security of peace [Acts 14:22].

That Luther's position as stated in the Ninety-five Theses involved more than technical and abstruse questions of theology can be seen in the reaction of the Holy Roman Emperor to Luther's proposed debate.

Maximilian's Letter to Leo X

Augsburg, August 5, 1518.

MOST BLESSED FATHER and most revered Lord! We have recently heard that a certain Augustinian Friar, Martin Luther by name, has published certain theses on indulgences to be discussed in the scholastic way, and that in these theses he has taught much on this subject and concerning the power of papal excommunication, part of which appears injurious and heretical, as has been noted by the Master of your sacred palace. This has displeased us the more because, as we are informed, the said friar obstinately adheres to his doctrine, and is said to have found several defenders of his errors among the great.

And as suspicious assertions and dangerous dogmas can be judged by no one better, more rightly and more truly than by your Holiness, who alone is able and ought to silence the authors of vain questions, sophisms and wordy quarrels, than which nothing more pestilent can happen to Christianity, for these men consider only how to magnify what they have taught, so your Holiness can maintain the sincere and solid doctrine approved by the consensus of the more learned opinion of the present age and of those who formerly died piously in Christ.

There is an ancient decree of the Pontifical College on the licensing of teachers, in which there is no provision whatever against sophistry, save in case the decretals are called in question, and whether it is right to teach that, the study of which has been disapproved by many and great authors.

Since, therefore, the authority of the Popes is disregarded, and doubtful, or rather erroneous opinions are alone received, it is bound to occur that those little fanciful and blind teachers should be led astray. And it is due to them that not only are many of the more solid doctors of the Church not only neglected, but even corrupted and mutilated.

We do not mention that these authors hatch many more heresies than were ever condemned. We do not mention that both Reuchlin's trial and the present most dangerous dispute about indulgences and papal censures have been brought forth by these pernicious authors. If the authority of your Holiness and of the most reverend fathers does not put an end to such doctrines, soon their authors will not only impose on the unlearned multitude, but will win the favor of princes, to their mutual destruction. If we shut our eyes and leave them the field open and free, it will happen, as they chiefly desire, that the whole world will be forced to look on their follies instead of on the best and most holy doctors.

Of our singular reverence for the Apostolic See, we have signified this to your Holiness, so that simple Christianity may not be injured and scandalized by these rash disputes and captious arguments. Whatever may be righteously decided upon in this our Empire, we will make all our subjects obey for the praise and honor of God Almighty and the salvation of Christians.

The reaction that followed the publication of his Ninety-five Theses forced Luther to define and defend his position in some detail. This he did in 1520 in the two treatises from which the following selections are taken. After their publication a reconciliation with Rome appeared doubtful.

FROM *Address to the Christian Nobility of the German Nation* BY *Martin Luther*

GRACE AND POWER FROM God, Most Illustrious Majesty, and most gracious and dear Lords.

It is not out of sheer forwardness or rashness that I, a single, poor man, have undertaken to address your worships. The distress and oppression which weigh down all the Estates of Christendom, especially of Germany, and which move not me alone, but everyone to cry out time and again, and to pray for help, have forced me even now to cry aloud that God may inspire some one with His Spirit to lend this suffering nation a helping hand. Ofttimes the councils have made some pretense at reformation, but their attempts have been cleverly hindered by the guile of certain men and things have gone from bad to worse. I now intend, by the help of God, to throw some light upon the wiles and wickedness of these men, to the end that when they are known, they may not henceforth be so hurtful and so great a hindrance. God has given us a noble youth to be our head and thereby has awakened great hopes of good in many hearts, wherefore it is meet that we should do our part and profitably use this time of grace.

In this whole matter the first and most important thing is that we take earnest heed not to enter on it trusting in great might or in human reason, even though all power in the world were ours; for God cannot and will not suffer a good work to be begun with trust in our own power or reason. Such works He crushes ruthlessly to earth, as it is written in the Thirty-third Psalm, "There is no king saved by the multitude of an host; a mighty man is not delivered by much strength." On this account, I fear, it came to pass of old that the good Emperors Frederick I and II and many other German emperors were shamefully oppressed and trodden under foot by the popes, although all the world feared them. It may be that they relied on their own might more than on God, and therefore they had to fall. In our own times, too, what was it that raised the bloodthirsty Julius II to such heights? Nothing else, I fear, except that France, the Germans and Venice relied upon themselves. The children of Benjamin slew 42,000 Israelites because the latter relied on their own strength.

That it may not so fare with us and our noble young Emperor Charles, we must be sure that in this matter we are dealing not with men, but with the princes of hell, who can fill the world with war and bloodshed, but whom war and bloodshed do not overcome. We must go at this work despairing of physical force and humbly trusting God; we must seek God's help with earnest prayer, and fix our minds on nothing else than the misery and distress of suffering Christendom, without regard to the deserts of evil men. Otherwise we may start the game with great prospect of success, but when we get well into it the evil spirits will stir up such confusion that the whole world will swim in blood, and yet nothing will come of it. Let us act wisely, therefore, and in the fear of God. The more force we use, the greater our disaster if we do not act humbly and in God's fear. The popes and the Romans have hitherto been able, by the devil's help, to set kings at odds with one another, and they may well be able to do it again, if we proceed by our own might and cunning, without God's help.

THE THREE WALLS OF THE ROMANISTS

The Romanists, with great adroitness, have built three walls about them, behind which they have hitherto defended themselves in such wise that no one has been able to reform them and this has been the cause of terrible corruption throughout all Christendom.

First, when pressed by the temporal power, they have made decrees and said that the temporal power has no jurisdiction over them, but, on the other hand, that the spiritual is above the temporal power. Second, when the attempt is made to reprove them out of the Scriptures, they raise the objection that the interpretation of the Scriptures belongs to no one except the pope. Third, if threatened with a council, they answer with the fable that no one can call a council but the pope.

In this wise they have slyly stolen from us our three rods, that they may go unpunished, and have ensconced themselves within the safe stronghold of these three walls, that they may practice all the knavery and wickedness which we now see. Even when they have been compelled to hold a council they have weakened its power in advance by previously binding the princes with an oath to let them remain as they are. Moreover, they have given the pope full authority over all the decisions of the council, so that it is all one whether there are many councils or no councils—except that they deceive us with puppet-shows and sham battles. So terribly do they fear for their skin in a really free council! And they have intimidated kings and princes by making them believe it would be an offense against God not to obey them in all these knavish, crafty deceptions.

Now God help us, and give us one of the trumpets with which the walls of Jericho were overthrown, that we may blow down these walls of straw and paper, and may set free the Christian rods of the punishment of sin, bringing to light the craft and deceit of the devil, to the end that through punishment we may reform ourselves, and once more attain God's favor.

Against the *first wall* we will direct our first attack.

It is pure invention that pope, bishops, priests and monks are to be called the "spiritual estate"; princes, lords, artisans and farmers the "temporal estate." That is indeed a fine bit of lying and hypocrisy. Yet no one should be frightened by it and for this reason—viz., that all Christians are truly of the "spiritual estate," and there is among them no difference at all but that of office, as Paul says in I Corinthians 12. We are all one body, yet every member has its own work, whereby it serves every other, all because we have one baptism, one Gospel, one faith, and are all alike Christians; for baptism, Gospel, and faith alone make us "spiritual" and a Christian people.

But that a pope or a bishop anoints, confers tonsures, ordains, consecrates, or prescribes dress unlike that of the laity—this may make hypocrites and graven images, but it never makes a Christian or "spiritual" man. Through baptism all of us are consecrated to the priesthood, as St. Peter says in I Peter 2, "Ye are a royal priesthood, a priestly kingdom," and the book of Revelation says, "Thou hast made us by thy blood to be priests and kings." For if we had no higher consecration than pope or bishop gives, the consecration by pope or bishop would never make a priest, nor might anyone either say mass or preach a sermon or give absolution. Therefore when the bishop consecrates it is the same thing as if he, in the place and stead of the whole congregation, all of whom have like power, were to take one out of their number and charge him to use this power for the others; just as though ten brothers, all king's sons and equal heirs, were to choose one of themselves to rule the inheritance for them all—they would all be kings and equal in power, though one of them would be charged with the duty of ruling.

To make it still clearer. If a little group of pious Christian laymen were taken captive and set down in a wilderness, and had among them no priest consecrated by a bishop, and if there in the wilderness they were to agree in choosing one of themselves, married or unmarried, and were to charge him with the office of baptizing, saying mass, absolving and preaching, such a man would be as truly a priest as though all bishops and popes had consecrated him. That is why in cases of necessity anyone can baptize and give absolution, which would be impossible unless we were all priests. This great grace and power of baptism and of the Christian Estate they have well-nigh destroyed and caused us to forget through the canon law. It was in the manner aforesaid that Christians in olden days chose from their number bishops and priests, who were afterwards confirmed by other bishops, without all the show which now obtains. It was thus that Sts. Augustine, Ambrose, and Cyprian became bishops.

Since, then, the temporal authorities are baptized with the same baptism and have the same faith and Gospel as we, we must grant that they are priests and bishops, and count their office one which has a proper and a useful place in the Christian community. For whoever comes out of the water of baptism can boast that he is already consecrated priest, bishop, and pope, though it is not seemly that everyone should exercise the office. Nay, just because we are all in like manner priests, no one must put himself forward and undertake, without our consent and election, to do what is in the power of all of us. For what is common to all, no one dare take upon himself without the will and the command of the community; and should it happen that one chosen for such an office were deposed for malfeasance, he would then be just what he was before he held office. Therefore a priest in Christendom is nothing else than an office-holder. While he is in office, he has precedence; when deposed, he is a peasant or a townsman like the rest. Beyond all doubt, then, a priest is no longer a priest when he is deposed. But now they have invented *characteres indelebiles*, and prate that a deposed priest is nevertheless something different from a mere layman. They even dream that a priest can never become a layman, or be anything else than a priest. All this is mere talk and man-made law.

From all this it follows that there is really no difference between laymen and priests, princes and bishops, "spirituals" and "temporals," as they call them, except that of office and work, but not of "estate"; for they are all of the same estate—true priests, bishops and popes— though they are not all engaged in the same work, just as all priests and monks have not the same work.

*   *   *

The *second wall* is still more flimsy and worthless. They wish to be the only Masters of the Holy Scriptures even though in all their lives they learn nothing from them. They assume for themselves sole authority, and with insolent juggling of words they would persuade us that the pope, whether he be a bad man or a good man, cannot err in matters of faith, and yet they cannot prove a single letter of it. Hence it comes that so many heretical and unchristian, nay, even unnatural ordinances have a place in the canon law, of which, however, there is no present need to speak. For since they think that the Holy Spirit never leaves them, be they never so unlearned and wicked, they make bold to decree whatever they will. And if it were true, where would be the need or use of the Holy Scriptures? Let us burn them, and be satisfied with the unlearned lords at Rome, who are possessed of the Holy Spirit—although He can possess only pious hearts! Unless I had read it myself, I could not have believed that the devil would make such clumsy pretensions at Rome, and find a following.

But not to fight them with mere words, we will quote the Scriptures. St. Paul says in I Corinthians 14: "If to anyone something better

is revealed, though he be sitting and listening to another in God's Word,
then the first, who is speaking, shall hold his peace and give place."
What would be the use of this commandment, if we were only to
believe him who does the talking or who has the highest seat? Christ
also says in John 6 that all Christians shall be taught of God. Thus it
may well happen that the pope and his followers are wicked men, and
no true Christians, not taught of God, not having true understanding.
On the other hand, an ordinary man may have true understanding;
why then should we not follow him? Has not the pope erred many
times? Who would help Christendom when the pope errs, if we were
not to believe another, who had the Scriptures on his side, more than
the pope?

Therefore it is a wickedly invented fable, and they cannot produce
a letter in defense of it, that the interpretation of Scripture or the confirmation of its interpretation belongs to the pope alone. They have
themselves usurped this power; and although they allege that this
power was given to Peter when the keys were given to him, it is plain
enough that the keys were not given to Peter alone, but to the whole
community. Moreover, the keys were not ordained for doctrine or government, but only for the binding and loosing of sin, and whatever
further power of the key they arrogate to themselves is mere invention. But Christ's word to Peter, "I have prayed for thee that thy
faith fail not," cannot be applied to the pope, since the majority of the
popes have been without faith, as they must themselves confess. Besides, it is not only for Peter that Christ prayed, but also for all
Apostles and Christians, as he says in John 17: "Father, I pray for
those whom thou hast given me, and not for these only, but for all who
believe on me through their word." It not this clear enough?

Only think of it yourself! They must confess that there are pious
Christians among us, who have the true faith, Spirit, understanding,
word, and mind of Christ. Why, then, should we reject their word and
understanding and follow the pope, who has neither faith nor Spirit?
That would be to deny the whole faith and the Christian Church.
Moreover, it is not the pope alone who is always in the right, if the
article of the Creed is correct: "I believe in one holy Christian Church";
otherwise the prayer must run: "I believe in the pope at Rome," and
so reduce the Christian Church to one man—which would be nothing
else than a devilish and hellish error.

Besides, if we were all priests, as was said above, and all have
one faith, one Gospel, one sacrament, why should we not also have
the power to test and judge what is correct or incorrect in matters of
faith? What becomes of the words of Paul in I Corinthians 2: "He
that is spiritual judgeth all things, yet he himself is judged of no man,"
and II Corinthians 4: "We have all the same Spirit of faith"? Why,
then, should not we perceive what squares with faith and what does
not, as well as does an unbelieving pope?

All these and many other texts should make us bold and free,
and we should not allow the Spirit of liberty, as Paul calls Him, to be
frightened off by the fabrications of the popes, but we ought to go
boldly forward to test all that they do or leave undone, according to

our interpretation of the Scriptures, which rests on faith, and compel them to follow not their own interpretation, but the one that is better. In the olden days Abraham had to listen to his Sarah, although she was in more complete subjection to him than we are to anyone on earth. Balaam's ass, also, was wiser than the prophet himself. If God then spoke by an ass against a prophet, why should He not be able even now to speak by a righteous man against the pope? In like manner St. Paul rebukes St. Peter as a man in error. Therefore it behooves every Christian to espouse the cause of the faith, to understand and defend it, and to rebuke all errors.

The *third wall* falls of itself when the first two are down. For when the pope acts contrary to the Scriptures, it is our duty to stand by the Scriptures, to reprove him, and to constrain him, according to the word of Christ in Matthew 18: "If thy brother sin against thee, go and tell it him between thee and him alone; if he hear thee not, then take with thee one or two more; if he hear them not, tell it to the Church; if he hear not the Church, consider him a heathen." Here every member is commanded to care for every other. How much rather should we do this when the member that does evil is a ruling member, and by his evil-doing is the cause of much harm and offense to the rest! But if I am to accuse him before the Church, I must bring the Church together.

They have no basis in Scripture for their contention that it belongs to the pope alone to call a council or confirm its actions; for this is based merely upon their own laws, which are valid only in so far as they are not injurious to Christendom or contrary to the laws of God. When the pope deserves punishment, such laws go out of force, since it is injurious to Christendom not to punish him by means of a council.

Thus we read in Acts 15 that it was not St. Peter who called the Apostolic Council, but the Apostles and elders. If, then, that right had belonged to St. Peter alone, the council would not have been a Christian council, but a heretical *conciliabulum*. Even the Council of Nicaea —the most famous of all—was neither called nor confirmed by the Bishop of Rome, but by the Emperor Constantine, and many other emperors after him did the like, yet these councils were the most Christian of all. But if the pope alone had the right to call councils, then all these councils must have been heretical. Moreover, if I consider the councils which the pope has created, I find that they have done nothing of special importance.

Therefore, when necessity demands, and the pope is an offense to Christendom, the first man who is able should, as a faithful member of the whole body, do what he can to bring about a truly free council. No one can do this so well as the temporal authorities, especially since now they also are fellow-Christians, fellow-priests, "fellow-spirituals," fellow-lords over all things, and whenever it is needful or profitable, they should give free course to the office and work in which God has put them above every man. Would it not be an unnatural thing, if a fire broke out in a city, and everybody were to stand by and let it burn on and on and consume everything that could burn, for the sole reason that nobody had the authority of the burgomaster, or because, perhaps, the fire broke out in the burgomaster's house? In such case is it not the duty of every citizen to arouse and call the rest? How much more should this be done in the spiritual city of Christ, if a fire of offense breaks out, whether in the papal government, or anywhere else? In the same way, if the enemy attacks a city, he who first rouses the others deserves honor and thanks; why then should he not deserve honor who makes known the presence of the enemy from hell, and awakens the Christians, and calls them together?

But all their boasts of an authority which dare not be opposed amount to nothing after all. No one in Christendom has authority to do injury, or to forbid the resisting of injury. There is no authority in the Church save for edification. Therefore, if the pope were to use his authority to prevent the calling of a free council, and thus became a hindrance to the edification of the Church, we should have regard neither for him nor for his authority; and if he were to hurl his bans and thunderbolts, we should despise his conduct as that of a madman, and relying on God, hurl back the ban on him, and coerce him as best we could. For this presumptuous authority of his is nothing; he has no such authority, and he is quickly overthrown by a text of Scripture; for Paul says to the Corinthians, "God has given us authority not for the destruction, but for the edification of Christendom." Who is ready to overlap this text? It is only the power of the devil and of Antichrist which resists the things that serve for the edification of Christendom; it is, therefore, in no wise to be obeyed, but is to be opposed with life and goods and all our strength.

FROM *A Treatise on Christian Liberty* BY *Martin Luther*

MANY HAVE THOUGHT CHRISTIAN faith to be an easy thing, and not a few have given it a place among the virtues. This they do because they have had no experience of it, and have never tasted what virtue there is in faith. For it is impossible that anyone should write well of it or well understand what is correctly written of it, unless he has at some time tasted the courage faith gives a man when trials oppress him. But he who has had even a faint taste of it can never write, speak, mediate, or hear enough concerning it. For it is a living fountain springing up into life everlasting, as Christ calls it in John 4. For my part, although I have no wealth of faith to boast of and know how scant my store is, yet I hope that, driven about by great and various temptations, I have attained to a little faith, and that I can speak of it, if not more elegantly, certainly more to the point, than those literalists and all too subtle disputants have hitherto done, who have not even understood what they have written.

That I may make the way easier for the unlearned—for only such do I serve—I set down first these two propositions concerning the liberty and the bondage of the spirit:

A Christian man is a perfectly free lord of all, subject to none.
A Christian man is a perfectly dutiful servant of all, subject to all.

Although these two theses seem to contradict each other, yet, if they should be found to fit together they would serve our purpose beautifully. For they are both Paul's own, who says, in I Corinthians 9, "Whereas I was free, I made myself the servant of all," and Romans 8, "Owe no man anything, but to love one another." Now love by its very nature is ready to serve and to be subject to him who is loved. So Christ, although Lord of all, was made of a woman, made under the law, and hence was at the same time free and a servant, at the same time in the form of God and in the form of a servant.

Let us start, however, with something more remote from our subject, but more obvious. Man has a twofold nature, a spiritual and a bodily. According to the spiritual nature, which men call the soul, he is called a spiritual, or inner, or new man; according to the bodily nature, which men call the flesh, he is called a carnal, or outward, or old man, of whom the Apostle writes, in 2 Corinthians 4, "Though our outward man is corrupted, yet the inward man is renewed day by day." Because of this diversity of nature the Scriptures assert contradictory things of the same man, since these two men in the same man contradict each other, since the flesh lusteth against the spirit and the spirit against the flesh (Galatians 5).

First, let us contemplate the inward man, to see how a righteous, free, and truly Christian man, that is, a new spiritual, inward man, comes into being. It is evident that no external thing, whatsoever it be, has any influence whatever in producing Christian righteousness or liberty, nor in producing unrighteousness or bondage. A simple argument will furnish the proof. What can it profit the soul if the body fare well, be free and active, eat, drink, and do as it pleases? For in these things even the most godless slaves of all the vices fare well. On the other hand, how will ill health or imprisonment or hunger or thirst or any other external misfortune hurt the soul? With these things even the most godly men are afflicted, and those who because of a clear conscience are most free. None of these things touch either the liberty or the bondage of the soul. The soul receives no benefit if the body is adorned with the sacred robes of the priesthood, or dwells in sacred places, or is occupied with sacred duties, or prays, fasts, abstains from certain kinds of food, or does any work whatsoever that can be done by the body and in the body. The righteousness and the freedom of the soul demand something far different, since the things which have been mentioned could be done by any wicked man, and such works produce nothing but hypocrites. On the other hand, it will not hurt the soul if the body is clothed in secular dress, dwells in unconsecrated places, eats and drinks as others do, does not pray aloud, and neglects to do all the things mentioned above, which hypocrites can do.

Further, to put aside all manner of works, even contemplation, meditation, and all that the soul can do, avail nothing. One thing and one only is necessary for Christian life, righteousness, and liberty. That one thing is the most holy Word of God, the Gospel of Christ, as he says, John 11, "I am the resurrection and the life: he that believeth in me shall not die forever"; and John 8, "If the Son shall make you free, you shall be free indeed"; and Matthew 4, "Not in bread alone doth man live; but in every word that proceedeth from the mouth of God." Let us then consider it certain and conclusively established that the soul can do without all things except the Word of God, and that where this is not there is no help for the soul in anything else whatever. But if it has the Word it is rich and lacks nothing, since this Word is the Word of life, of truth, of light, of peace, of righteousness, of salvation, of joy, of liberty, of wisdom, of power, of grace, of glory, and of every blessing beyond our power to estimate. This is why the prophet in the entire One Hundred and Nineteenth Psalm, and in many other places of Scripture, with so many sighs yearns after the Word of God and applies so many names to it. On the other hand, there is no more terrible plague with which the wrath of God can smite men than a famine of the hearing of His Word, as He says in Amos, just as there is no greater mercy than when He sends forth His Word, as we read in Psalm 107, "He sent His word and healed them, and delivered them from their destructions." Nor was Christ sent into the world for any other ministry but that of the Word, and the whole spiritual estate, apostles, bishops and all the priests, has been called and instituted only for the ministry of the Word.

You ask, "What then is this Word of God, and how shall it be used, since there are so many words of God?" I answer, the Apostle explains that in Romans 1. The Word is the Gospel of God concerning His Son, who was made flesh, suffered, rose from the dead, and was glorified through the Spirit who sanctifies. For to preach Christ means to feed the soul, to make it righteous, to set it free, and to save it, if it believe the preaching. For faith alone is the saving and efficacious use of the Word of God, Romans 10, "If thou confess with thy mouth that Jesus is Lord, and believe with thy heart that God hath raised Him up from the dead, thou shalt be saved"; and again, "The end of the law is Christ, unto righteousness to everyone that believeth"; and, in Romans 1, "The just shall live by his faith." The Word of God cannot be received and cherished by any works whatever, but only by faith. Hence it is clear that, as the soul needs only the Word for its life and righteousness, so it is justified by faith alone and not by any works; for if it could be justified by anything else, it would not need the Word, and therefore it would not need faith. But this faith cannot at all exist in connection with works, that is to say, if you at the same time claim to be justified by works, whatever their character; for that would be to halt between two sides, to worship Baal and to kiss the hand, which, as Job says, is a very great iniquity. Therefore the moment you begin to believe, you learn that all things in you are altogether blameworthy, sinful, and damnable, as Romans 3 says, "For all have sinned and lack the glory of God"; and again, "There is none just, there is none that doeth good, all have turned out of the way: they are become unprofitable together." When you have learned this, you will know that you need Christ, who suffered and rose again for you, that, believing in Him, you may through this faith become a new man, in that all your sins are forgiven, and you are justified by the merits of another, namely, of Christ alone.

Since, therefore, this faith can rule only in the inward man, as Romans 10 says, "With the heart we believe unto righteousness"; and since faith alone justifies, it is clear that the inward man cannot be justified, made free, and be saved by any outward work or dealing whatsoever, and that works, whatever their character, have nothing to do with this inward man. On the other hand, only ungodliness and unbelief of heart, and no outward work, make him guilty and a damnable servant of sin. Wherefore it ought to be the first concern of every Christian to lay aside all trust in works, and more and more to strengthen faith alone, and through faith to grow in the knowledge, not of works, but of Christ Jesus, who suffered and rose for him, as Peter teaches, in the last chapter of his first Epistle; since no other work makes a Christian. Thus when the Jews asked Christ, John 6, what they should do that they might work the works of God, He brushed aside the multitude of works in which He saw that they abounded, and enjoined upon them a single work, saying, "This is the work of God, that you believe in Him whom He hath sent. For him hath God the Father sealed."

Luther's declaration of theological independence was made at Worms in 1521. He had been summoned there to appear before the emperor and appropriate members of the church hierarchy to defend himself against the charge of heresy. The break with Rome now became irrevocable.

Speech Before Emperor Charles by *Martin Luther*

"MOST SERENE EMPEROR, most illustrious princes, most clement lords, obedient to the time set for me yesterday evening, I appear before you, beseeching you, by the mercy of God, that your most serene majesty and your most illustrious lordships may deign to listen graciously to this my cause—which is, as I hope, a cause of justice and of truth. If through my inexperience I have either not given the proper titles to some, or have offended in some manner against court customs and etiquette, I beseech you to kindly pardon me, as a man accustomed not to courts but to the cells of monks. I can bear no other witness about myself but that I have taught and written up to this time with simplicity of heart, as I had in view only the glory of God and the sound instruction of Christ's faithful.

"Most serene emperor, most illustrious princes, concerning those questions proposed to me yesterday on behalf of your serene majesty, whether I acknowledged as mine the books enumerated and published in my name and whether I wished to persevere in their defense or to retract them, I have given to the first question my full and complete answer, in which I still persist and shall persist forever. These books are mine and they have been published in my name by me, unless in the meantime, either through the craft or the mistaken wisdom of my emulators, something in them has been changed or wrongly cut out. For plainly I cannot acknowledge anything except what is mine alone and what has been written by me alone, to the exclusion of all interpretations of anyone at all.

"In replying to the second question, I ask that your most serene majesty and your lordships may deign to note that my books are not all of the same kind.

"For there are some in which I have discussed religious faith and morals simply and evangelically, so that even my enemies themselves are compelled to admit that these are useful, harmless, and clearly worthy to be read by Christians. Even the bull, although harsh and cruel, admits that some of my books are inoffensive, and yet allows these also to be condemned with a judgment which is utterly monstrous. Thus, if I should begin to disavow them, I ask you, what would I be doing? Would not I, alone of all men, be condemning the very truth upon which friends and enemies equally agree, striving alone against the harmonious confession of all?

"Another group of my books attacks the papacy and the affairs of the papist as those who both by their doctrines and very wicked examples have laid waste the Christian world with evil that affects the spirit and the body. For no one can deny or conceal this fact, when the experience of all and the complaints of everyone witness that through the decrees of the pope and the doctrines of men the consciences of the faithful have been most miserably entangled, tortured, and torn to pieces. Also, property and possessions, especially in this illustrious nation of Germany, have been devoured by an unbelievable tyranny and are being devoured to this time without letup and by unworthy means. [Yet the papists] by their own decrees (as in dist. 9 and 25; ques. 1 and 2) warn that the papal laws and doctrines which are contrary to the gospel or the opinions of the fathers are to be regarded as erroneous and reprehensible. If, therefore, I should have retracted these writings, I should have done nothing other than to have added strength to this [papal] tyranny and I should have opened not only windows but doors to such great godlessness. It would rage farther and more freely than ever it has dared up to this time. Yes, from the proof of such a revocation on my part, their wholly lawless and unrestrained kingdom of wickedness would become still more intolerable for the already wretched people; and their rule would be further strengthened and established, especially if it should be reported that this evil deed had been done by me by virtue of the authority of your most serene majesty and of the whole Roman Empire. Good God! What a cover for wickedness and tyranny I should have then become.

"I have written a third sort of book against some private and (as they say) distinguished individuals—those, namely, who strive to preserve the Roman tyranny and to destroy the godliness taught by me.

Against these I confess I have been more violent than my religion or profession demands. But then, I do not set myself up as a saint; neither am I disputing about my life, but about the teaching of Christ. It is not proper for me to retract these works, because by this retraction it would again happen that tyranny and godlessness would, with my patronage, rule and rage among the people of God more violently than ever before.

"However, because I am a man and not God, I am not able to shield my books with any other protection than that which my Lord Jesus Christ himself offered for his teaching. When questioned before Annas about his teaching and struck by a servant, he said: 'If I have spoken wrongly, bear witness to the wrong' [John 18:19–23]. If the Lord himself, who knew that he could not err, did not refuse to hear testimony against his teaching, even from the lowliest servant, how much more ought I, who am the lowest scum and able to do nothing except err, desire and expect that somebody should want to offer testimony against my teaching! Therefore, I ask by the mercy of God, may your most serene majesty, most illustrious lordships, or anyone at all who is able, either high or low, bear witness, expose my errors, overthrowing them by the writings of the prophets and the evangelists. Once I have been taught I shall be quite ready to renounce every error, and I shall be the first to cast my books into the fire.

"From these remarks I think it is clear that I have sufficiently considered and weighed the hazards and dangers, as well as the excitement and dissensions aroused in the world as a result of any teachings, things about which I was gravely and forcefully warned yesterday. To see excitement and dissension arise because of the Word of God is to me clearly the most joyful aspect of all in these matters. For this is the way, the opportunity, and the result of the Word of God, just as He [Christ] said, 'I have not come to bring peace, but a sword. For I have come to set a man against his father, etc.' [Matt. 10:34–35]. Therefore, we ought to think how marvelous and terrible is our God in his counsels, lest by chance what is attempted for settling strife grows rather into an intolerable deluge of evils, if we begin by condemning the Word of God. And concern must be shown lest the reign of this most noble youth, Prince Charles (in whom after God is our great hope), become unhappy and inauspicious. I could illustrate this with abundant examples from Scripture—like Pharaoh, the king of Babylon, and the kings of Israel who, when they endeavored to pacify and strengthen their kingdoms by the wisest counsels, most surely destroyed themselves. For it is He who takes the wise in their own craftiness [Job 5:13] and overturns mountains before they know it [Job 9:5]. Therefore we must fear God. I do not say these things because there is a need of either my teachings or my warnings for such leaders as you, but because I must not withhold the allegiance which I owe my Germany. With these words I commend myself to your most serene majesty and to your lordships, humbly asking that I not be allowed through the agitation of my enemies, without cause, to be made hateful to you. I have finished."

When I had finished, the speaker for the emperor said, as if in reproach, that I had not answered the question, that I ought not call into question those things which had been condemned and defined in councils; therefore what was sought from me was not a horned response, but a simple one, whether or not I wished to retract.

Here I answered:

"Since then your serene majesty and your lordships seek a simple answer, I will give it in this manner, neither horned nor toothed: Unless I am convinced by the testimony of the Scriptures or by clear reason (for I do not trust either in the pope or in councils alone, since it is well known that they have often erred and contradicted themselves), I am bound by the Scriptures I have quoted and my conscience is captive to the Word of God. I cannot and I will not retract anything, since it is neither safe nor right to go against conscience.

"I cannot do otherwise, here I stand, may God help me, Amen."

4 *The Problem of Martin Luther*

Erik Erikson of Harvard University is a leader of contemporary psychiatric thought. In his book Young Man Luther *he attempts to account for Luther's actions in terms of modern depth psychology.*

FROM *Young Man Luther* BY *Erik H. Erikson*

I HAVE CALLED THE MAJOR crisis of adolescence the *identity crisis*; it occurs in that period of the life cycle when each youth must forge for himself some central perspective and direction, some working unity, out of the effective remnants of his childhood and the hopes of his anticipated adulthood; he must detect some meaningful resemblance between what he has come to see in himself and what his sharpened awareness tells him others judge and expect him to be. This sounds dangerously like common sense; like all health, however, it is a matter of course only to those who possess it, and appears as a most complex achievement to those who have tasted its absence. Only in ill health does one realize the intricacy of the body; and only in a crisis, individual or historical, does it become obvious what a sensitive combination of interrelated factors the human personality is—a combination of capacities created in the distant past and of opportunities divined in the present; a combination of totally unconscious preconditions developed in individual growth and of social conditions created and re-created in the precarious interplay of generations. In some young people, in some classes, at some periods in history, this crisis will be minimal; in other people, classes, and periods, the crisis will be clearly marked off as a critical period, a kind of "second birth," apt to be aggravated either by widespread neuroticisms or by pervasive ideological unrest. Some young individuals will succumb to this crisis in all manner of neurotic, psychotic, or delinquent behavior; others will resolve it through participation in ideological movements passionately concerned with religion or politics, nature or art. Still others, although suffering and deviating dangerously through what appears to be a prolonged adolescence, eventually come to contribute an original bit to an emerging style of life: the very danger which they have sensed has forced them to mobilize capacities to see and say, to dream and plan, to design and construct, in new ways.

Luther, so it seems, at one time was a rather endangered young man, beset with a syndrome of conflicts whose outline we have learned to recognize, and whose components to analyse. He found a spiritual solution, not without the well-timed help of a therapeutically clever superior in the Augustinian order. His solution roughly bridged a political and psychological vacuum which history had created in a significant portion of Western Christendom. Such coincidence, if further coinciding with the deployment of highly specific personal gifts, makes for historical "greatness." We will follow Luther through the crisis of his youth, and the unfolding of his gifts, to the first manifestation of his originality as a thinker, namely, to the emergence of a new theology, apparently not immediately perceived as a radical innovation either by him or his listeners, in his first Lectures on the Psalms (1513). What happened to him after he had acquired a historical identity is more than another chapter; for even half of the man is too much for one book. The difference between the young and the old Luther is so marked, and the second, the sturdy orator, so exclusive a Luther-image to most readers, that I will speak of "Martin" when I report on Luther's early years, which according to common usage in the Luther literature include his twenties; and of "Luther" where and when he has become the leader of Lutherans, seduced by history into looking back on his past as upon a mythological autobiography.

Kierkegaard's remark has a second part: ". . . of very great import for Christendom." This calls for an investigation of how the individual "case" became an important, an historic "event," and for formulations concerning the spiritual and political identity crisis of Northern Christendom in Luther's time. True, I could have avoided those methodological uncertainties and impurities which will undoubtedly occur by sticking to my accustomed job of writing a case history, and leaving the historical event to those who, in turn, would consider the case a mere accessory to the event. But we clinicians have learned in recent years that we cannot lift a case history out of history, even as we suspect that historians, when they try to separate the logic of the historic event from that of the life histories which intersect in it, leave a number of vital historical problems unattended. So we may have to risk that bit of impurity which is inherent in the hyphen of the psycho-historical as well as of all other hyphenated approaches. They are the compost heap of today's interdisciplinary efforts, which may help to fertilize new fields, and to produce future flowers of new methodological clarity.

*   *   *

We cannot leave history entirely to nonclinical observers and to professional historians who often all too nobly immerse themselves into the very disguises, rationalizations, and idealizations of the historical process from which it should be their business to separate themselves. Only when the relation of historical forces to the basic functions and stages of the mind has been jointly charted and understood can we begin a psychoanalytic critique of society as such without falling back into mystical or moralistic philosophizing.

Freud warned against the possible misuse of his work as an ideology, a *"Weltanschauung"*; but as we shall see in Luther's life and work, a man who inspires new ideas has little power to restrict them to the area of his original intentions. And Freud himself did not refrain from interpreting other total approaches to man's condition, such as religion, as consequences of man's inability to shake off the bonds of his prolonged childhood, and thus comparable to collective neuroses.

The psychological and historical study of the religious crisis of a young great man renews the opportunity to review this assertion in the light of ego-psychology and of theories of psychosocial development.

*　　*　　*

In what follows, themes from Luther's first lectures are discussed side by side with psychoanalytic insights. Theological readers will wonder whether Luther saved theology from philosophy only to have it exploited by psychology; while psychoanalysts may suspect me of trying to make space for a Lutheran God in the structure of the psyche. My purposes, however, are more modest: I intend to demonstrate that Luther's redefinition of man's condition—while part and parcel of his theology—has striking configurational parallels with inner dynamic shifts like those which clinicians recognize in the recovery of individuals from psychic distress. In brief, I will try to indicate that Luther, in laying the foundation for a "religiosity for the adult man," displayed the attributes of his own hard-won adulthood; his renaissance of faith portrays a vigorous recovery of his own ego-initiative. To indicate this I will focus on three ideas: the affirmation of voice and word as the instruments of faith; the new recognition of God's "face" in the passion of Christ; and the redefinition of a just life.

After 1505 Luther had made no bones about the pernicious influence which "rancid Aristotelianism" had had on theology. Scholasticism had made him lose faith, he said; through St. Paul he had recovered it. He put the problem in terms of organ modes, by describing scholastic disputations as *dentes* and *linguae*: the teeth are hard and sinister, and form words in anger and fury; the tongue is soft and suavely persuasive. Using these modes, the devil can evoke purely intellectual mirages (*mira potest suggere in intellectu*). But the organ through which the word enters to replenish the heart is the ear (*natura enim verbi est audiri*), for it is in the nature of the word that it should be heard. On the other hand, faith comes from listening, not from looking (*quia est auditu fides, non ex visu*). Therefore, the greatest thing one can say about Christ, and about all Christians, is that they have *aures perfectas et perfossas*: good and open ears. But only what is perceived at the same time as a matter *affectionalis* and *moralis* as well as intellectual can be a matter sacred and divine: one must, therefore, hear before one sees, believe before one understands, be captivated before one captures. *Fides est "locus" animae*: faith is the seat, the organ of the soul. This had certainly been said before; but Luther's emphasis is not on Augustinian "infusion," or on a nominalist "obedience," but, in a truly Renaissance approach, on a self-verification through a God-given inner "apparatus." This *locus*, this apparatus, has its own way of seeking and searching—and it succeeds insofar as it develops its own *passivity*.

Paradoxically, many a young man (and son of a stubborn one) becomes a great man in his own sphere only by learning that deep passivity which permits him to let the data of his competency speak to him. As Freud said in a letter to Fliess, "I must wait until it moves in me so that I can perceive it: *bis es sich in mir ruehrt und ich davon erfahre.*" This may sound feminine, and, indeed, Luther bluntly spoke of an attitude of womanly conception—*sicut mulier in conceptu.* Yet it is clear that men call such attitudes and modes feminine only because the strain of paternalism has alienated us from them; for these modes are any organism's birthright, and all our partial as well as our total functioning is based on a metabolism of passivity and activity. Mannish man always wants to pretend that he made himself, or at any rate, that no simple woman bore him, and many puberty rites (consider the rebirth from a kiva in the American Southwest) dramatize a new birth from a spiritual mother of a kind that only men understand.

The theology as well as the psychology of Luther's passivity is that of man in the *state of prayer*, a state in which he fully means what he can say only to God: *Tibi soli peccavi*, I have sinned, not in relation to any person or institution, but in relation only to God, to *my* God.

In two ways, then, rebirth by prayer is passive: it means surrender to God the Father; but it also means to be reborn *ex matrice scripturae nati*: out of the matrix of the scriptures. "Matrix" is as close as such a man's man will come to saying "mater." But he cannot remember and will not acknowledge that long before he had developed those wilful modes which were specifically suppressed and paradoxically aggravated by a challenging father, a mother had taught him to touch the world with his searching mouth and his probing senses. What to a man's man, in the course of his development, seems like a passivity hard to acquire, is only a regained ability to be active with his oldest and most neglected modes. Is it coincidence that Luther, now that he was explicitly teaching passivity, should come to the conclusion that a lecturer should feed his audience as a mother suckles her child? Intrinsic to the kind of passivity we speak of is not only the memory of having been given, but also the identification with the maternal giver: "the glory of a good thing is that it flows out to others." I think that in the Bible Luther at last found a mother whom he could acknowledge: he could attribute to the Bible a generosity to which he could open himself, and which he could pass on to others, at last a mother's son.

Luther did use the words *passiva* and *passivus* when he spoke Latin, and the translation *passive* must be accepted as correct. But in German he often used the word *passivisch*, which is more actively passive, as passific would be. I think that the difference between the old modalities of *passive* and *active* is really that between *erleben* and *handeln*, of being in the state of *experiencing* or of *acting*. Meaningful implications are lost in the flat word *passivity*—among them the total attitude of living receptively and through the senses, of willingly "suffering" the voice of one's intuition and of living a *Passion*: that total passivity in which man regains, through considered self-sacrifice and self-transcendence, his active position in the face of nothingness, and thus is saved. Could this be one of the psychological riddles in the wisdom of the "foolishness of the cross"?

To Luther, the preaching and the praying man, the measure in depth of the perceived presence of the Word was the reaction with a total affect which leaves no doubt that one "means it." It may seem paradoxical to speak of an affect that one could not thus mean; yet it is obvious that rituals, observances, and performances do evoke transitory affects which can be put on for the occasion and afterward hung in the closet with one's Sunday clothes. Man is able to ceremonialize, as he can "automatize" psychologically, the signs and behaviors that are born of the deepest reverence or despair; however, for an affect to have a deep and lasting effect, or, as Luther would say, be *affectionalis* and *moralis*, it must not only be experienced as nearly overwhelming, but it must also in some way be affirmed by the ego as valid, almost as chosen: one means the affect, it signifies something meaningful, it is significant. Such is the relative nature of our ego and of our conscience that when the ego regains its composure after the auditory condemnation of the absolutist voice of conscience we mean what we have learned to believe, and our affects become those of positive conscience: faith, conviction, authority, indignation—all subjective states which are attributes of a strong sense of identity and, incidentally, are indispensable tools for strengthening identity in others. Luther speaks of matters of faith as experiences from which one will profit to the degree to which they were intensive and expressive (*quanto expressius et intensius*). If they are more *frigidus*, however, they are not merely a profit missed, they are a terrible deficit confirmed: for man without intense convictions is a robot with destructive techniques.

It is easy to see that these formulations, once revolutionary, are the commonplaces of today's pulpits. They are the bases of that most inflated of all oratorial currency, credal protestation in church and lecture hall, in political propaganda and in oral advertisement: the protestation, made to order for the occasion, that truth is only that which one means with one's whole being, and lives every moment. We, the heirs of Protestantism, have made convention and pretense out of the very sound of meaning it. What started with the German *Brustton der Ueberzeugung*, the manly chestiness of conviction, took many forms of authoritative appeal, the most recent one being the cute sincerity of our TV announcers. All this only indicates that Luther was a pioneer on one of our eternal inner frontiers, and that his struggle must continue (as any great man's must) exactly at that point where his word is perverted in his own name.

Psychotherapists, professional listeners and talkers in the sphere of affectivity and morality know only too well that man seldom really knows what he really means; he as often lies by telling the truth as he reveals the truth when he tries to lie. This is a psychological statement; and the psychoanalytic method, when it does not pretend to deliver complete honesty, over a period of time reveals approximately what somebody really means. But the center of the problem is simply this: in truly significant matters people, and especially children, have a devastatingly clear if mostly unconscious perception of what other people really mean, and sooner or later royally reward real love or take well-aimed revenge for implicit hate. Families in which each member is separated from the others by asbestos walls of verbal propriety, overt sweetness, cheap frankness, and rectitude tell one another off and talk back to each other with minute and unconscious displays of affect—not to mention physical complaints and bodily ailments—with which they worry, accuse, undermine, and murder one another.

Meaning it, then, is not a matter of credal protestation; verbal explicitness is not a sign of faith. Meaning it, means to be at one with an ideology in the process of rejuvenation; it implies a successful sublimation of one's libidinal strivings; and it manifests itself in a liberated craftsmanship.

When Luther listened to the scriptures he did not do so with an unprejudiced ear. His method of making an unprejudiced approach consisted of listening both ways—to the Word coming from the book and to the echo in himself. "Whatever is in your disposition," he said, "that the word of God will be unto you." Disposition here means the inner configuration of your most meant meanings. He knew that he meant it when he could say it: the spoken Word was the activity appropriate for his kind of passivity. Here "faith and word become one, an invincible whole." *"Der Glaub und das Worth wirth gantz ein Ding und ein unuberwintlich ding."*

Twenty-five times in the Lectures on the Psalms, against once in the Lectures on the Romans, Luther quotes two corresponding passages from Paul's first Epistle to the Corinthians. The first passage:

22. For the Jews require a sign, and the Greeks seek after wisdom;
23. But we preach Christ crucified, unto the Jews a stumblingblock, and unto the Greeks foolishness;
25. Because the foolishness of God is wiser than men; and the weakness of God is stronger than men.

This paradoxical foolishness and weakness of God became a theological absolute for Luther: there is not a word in the Bible, he exclaimed, which is *extra crucem*, which can be understood without reference to the cross; and this is all that shall and can be understood, as Paul had said in the other passage:

1. And I, brethren, when I came to you, came not with excellency of speech or of wisdom, declaring unto you the testimony of God.
2. For I determined not to know any thing among you, save Jesus Christ, and him crucified.
3. And I was with you in weakness, and in fear, and in much trembling.

Thus Luther abandoned any theological quibbling about the cross. He did not share St. Augustine's opinion that when Christ on the cross exclaimed *Deus meus, quare me derelequisti*, He had not been really abandoned, for as God's son and as God's word, He *was* God. Luther could not help feeling that St. Paul came closer to the truth when he assumed an existential paradox rather than a platonic fusion of essences; he insists on Christ's complete sense of abandonment and on his sincere and active premeditation in visiting hell. Luther spoke here in passionate terms very different from those of medieval adoration. He spoke of a man who was unique in all creation, yet lives in each man; and who is dying *in* everyone even as he died *for* everyone. It is clear that Luther rejected all arrangements by which an assortment of saints made it unnecessary for man to embrace the maximum of his own existential suffering. What he had tried, so desperately and for so long, to counteract and overcome he now accepted as his divine gift— the sense of utter abandonment, *sicut jam damnatus*, as if already in hell. The worst temptation, he now says, is not to have any; one can be sure that God is most angry when He does not seem angry at all. Luther warns of all those well-meaning (*bone intentionarii*) religionists who encourage man "to do what he can": to forestall sinning by clever planning; to seek redemption by observing all occasions for rituals, not forgetting to bring cash along to the limit of their means; and to be secure in the feeling that they are as humble and as peaceful as "it is in them to be." Luther, instead, made a virtue out of what his superiors had considered a vice in him (and we, a symptom), namely, the determined search for the rock bottom of his sinfulness: only thus, he says, can man judge himself as God would: *conformis deo est et verax et justus*. One could consider such conformity utter passivity in the face of God's judgment; but note that it really is an active self-observation, which scans the frontier of conscience for the genuine sense of guilt. Instead of accepting some impersonal and mechanical absolution, it insists on dealing with sincere guilt, perceiving as "God's judgment" what in fact is the individual's own truly meant self-judgment.

Is all this an aspect of personal adjustment to be interpreted as a set of unconscious tricks? Martin the son, who on a personal level had suffered deeply because he could not coerce his father into approving his religiosity as genuine, and who had borne with him the words of this father with an unduly prolonged filial obedience, assumes now on a religious level a volitional role toward filial suffering, perhaps making out of his protracted sonhood the victory of his Christlikeness. In his first Mass, facing the altar—the Father in heaven—and at the same time waiting to face his angry earthly father, Martin had "overlooked" a passage concerning Christ's mediatorship. Yet now, in finding Christ in himself, he establishes an inner position which goes beyond that of a neurotic compromise identification. He finds the core of a praying man's identity, and advances Christian ideology by an important step. It is clear that Luther abandoned the appreciation of Christ as a substitute who has died "for"—in the sense of "instead of"—us; he also abandoned the concept of Christ as an ideal figure to be imitated, or abjectly venerated, or ceremonially remembered as an event in the past. Christ now becomes the core of the Christian's identity: *quotidianus Christi adventus*, Christ is today here, in me. The affirmed passivity of suffering becomes the daily Passion and the Passion is the substitution of the primitive sacrifice of others with a most active, most masterly, affirmation of man's nothingness—which, by his own masterly choice, becomes his existential identity.

The men revered by mankind as saviors face and describe in lasting words insights which the ordinary man must avoid with all possible self-deception and exploitation of others. These men prove their voices which radiate to the farthest corner of their world and out into the millennia. Their passion contains elements of choice, mastery, and victory, and sooner or later earns them the name of King of Kings; their crown of thorns later becomes their successor's tiara. For a little while Luther, this first revolutionary individualist, saved the Saviour from the tiaras and the ceremonies, the hierarchies and the thought-police, and put him back where he arose: in each man's soul.

Is this not the counterpart, on the level of conscience, to Renaissance anthropocentrism? Luther left the heavens to science and restricted himself to what he could know of his own suffering and faith, that is, to what he could mean. He who had sought to dispel the angry cloud that darkened the face of the fathers and of The Father now said that Christ's life *is* God's face: *qui est facies patris*. The Passion is all that man can know of God: his conflicts, duly faced, are all that he can know of himself. The last judgment is the always present self-judgment. Christ did not live and die in order to make man poorer in the fear of his future judgment, but in order to make him abundant today: *nam judicia sunt ipsae passiones Christi quae in nobis abundant.* Look, Luther said at one point in these lectures (IV, 87), how everywhere painters depict Christ's passion as if they agreed with St. Paul that we know nothing but Christ crucified. The artist closest to Luther in spirit was Dürer, who etched his own face into Christ's countenance.

Gordon Rupp's discussion of the critical psychological period in Luther's life provides a historical counterweight to Erikson's reading of Luther's psychology.

FROM *The Righteousness of God* BY *Gordon Rupp*

WE DO NOT KNOW WHEN Luther began to study the Bible, though he must have begun his novitiate by learning portions of scripture which he would recite in the divine offices. It is certain that it became for him an all-important and absorbing study, until his mind was impregnated with the words and themes of the Bible, and he could handle the Biblical material with a facility which was the envy of his enemies, and with a frequent penetration into the exactness of Biblical vocabulary which modern Biblical scholarship has confirmed. But if the Bible was soon to become paramount with him, beyond Augustine and the Fathers, it was initially the meeting-place of all his problems, concentrated in one word. Here is his testimony, in the autobiographical preface which he wrote, at the end of his life (1545), before the Wittenberg edition of his Latin works. After rehearsing his career down to the year 1519, he pauses, and there follows this statement:

"Meanwhile then, in that year (1519), I turned once more to interpret the Psalms, relying on the fact that I was the more expert after I had handled in the schools the letters of St. Paul to the Romans and the Galatians, and that which is to the Hebrews. Certainly I had been seized with a greater ardour to understand Paul in the Epistle to the Romans (captus fueram cognoscendi), but as Virgil says, it was not 'coldness of the blood' which held me up until now, but one word (unicum vocabulum), that is, chapter 1. 'The Justice of God is revealed in it' (Justitia Dei). For I hated this word (vocabulum istud) 'Justitia Dei' which by the use and consent of all doctors I was taught (usu et consuetudine omnium doctorum doctus eram) to understand philosophically of that formal or active justice (as they call it) with which God is just, and punishes unjust sinners.

"For, however irreproachably I lived as a monk, I felt myself in the presence of God (coram Deo) to be a sinner with a most unquiet conscience nor could I trust that I had pleased him with my satisfaction. I did not love, nay, rather I hated this just God who punished sinners and if not with 'open blasphemy' certainly with huge murmuring I was angry with God, saying: 'As though it really were not enough that miserable sinners should be eternally damned with original sin, and have all kinds of calamities laid upon them by the law of the ten commandments, God must go and add sorrow upon sorrow and even through the Gospel itself bring his Justice and his Wrath to bear!' I raged in this way with a fierce and disturbed conscience, and yet I knocked importunately at Paul in this place, thirsting most ardently to know what St. Paul meant.

"At last, God being merciful, as I meditated day and night on the connection of the words, namely, 'the Justice of God is revealed in it, as it is written, "the Just shall live by Faith," ' there I began to understand the Justice of God as that by which the just lives by the gift of God, namely by faith, and this sentence, 'the Justice of God is revealed in the gospel,' to be that passive justice, with which the merciful God justifies us, by faith, as it is written 'The just lives by faith.'

"This straightway made me feel as though reborn, and as though I had entered through open gates into paradise itself. From then on, the whole face of scripture appeared different. I ran through the scriptures then, as memory served, and found the same analogy in other words, as the Work of God (opus) that which God works in us, Power of God (virtus Dei) with which he makes us strong, wisdom of God (sapientia Dei) with which he makes us wise, fortitude of God, salvation of God, glory of God.

"And now, as much as I had hated this word 'Justice of God' before, so much the more sweetly I extolled this word to myself now, so that this place in Paul was to me as a real gate of paradise. Afterwards, I read Augustine, 'On the Spirit and the Letter,' where beyond hope I found that he also similarly interpreted the Justice of God: that with which God endues us, when he justifies us. And although this were said imperfectly, and he does not clearly explain about 'imputation,' yet it pleased me that he should teach a Justice of God with which we are justified.

"Armed with these cogitations I began to interpret the Psalms again."

The narrative is in the main straightforward, and most of it can be checked against quotations already cited in these pages. But there are certain problems which must be faced. In the first place, to what period of his career does Luther refer when he speaks of his discovery about "Justitia Dei"? A superficial reading might suggest that he refers to the year (1519), when "armed with these cogitations" he began the second course of lectures on the Psalms. But it can be demonstrated that Luther had developed his teaching on this subject in these terms, at least by the time of his lectures on Romans (1515–16). The notion of a dislocation of the text, that refuge of desperate scholars, put forward by A. V. Müller, has no documentary evidence to support it, and as K. Holl pointed out, would make Luther commit grammatical solecisms. The suggestion that Luther in his old age made a slip of memory and confused his first and second lectures on the Psalms is hardly more convincing. Stracke has made a careful examination of the whole of this autobiographical fragment, and Luther emerges surprisingly well from the test. After thirty years, he is not unnaturally a month or two out here and there, gets a detail misplaced now and again, but when we remember that famous edition of the letters of Erasmus, which had more than half the dates wrong, and some of them years out, we can count this preface yet another disproof of the legend of Luther's anecdotage.

In fact, as Stracke pointed out, Luther's use of the phrase "captus fueram" makes perfectly tenable the interpretation that Luther has gone back in his reflection to an earlier period. Before attempting to identify this date more precisely, we must discuss the authenticity of the statement as a whole.

To impugn this was intended as a crowning demonstration of Denifle's "Luther und Luthertum." Denifle brought forward, in an appendix, a catena of 360 pages, giving the exposition of Rom. 1:17 by sixty doctors of the Western Church, which, he said, demonstrated beyond a doubt "not a single writer from the time of Ambrosiaster to the time of Luther understood this passage (Rom. 1:17) in the sense of the justice of God which punishes, of an angry God. All, on the contrary, have understood it of the God who justifies, the justice obtained by faith." Here, then, is the dilemma. Either Luther was a fool, or he was a liar. Either he was a bragging incompetent, boasting in his senility, or he was adding the last untruth to a long series of lying inventions. For Denifle, the two conclusions were not mutually exclusive.

Denifle included in the demonstration passages from the recently rediscovered lectures of Luther on Romans. This was intended as proof that Luther himself had used the supposed newly discovered meaning at a time anterior to 1515.

That part of his argument falls to the ground if we suppose Luther in fact to have spoken of a period before 1515. We may, therefore, re-sharpen Denifle's usefulness as an advocatus diaboli at this point, and present polemic with an argument here which, as far as we know, has been little noticed. In the Sentences of Peter Lombard, on which Luther lectured in 1509, and in the famous Dist. XVII of Book 1, to which, as we have seen, Luther paid special attention, there is imbedded a quotation from St. Augustine's "Spirit and Letter" which gives the so-called "passive" interpretation of "Justitia Dei":

"The love of God is said to be shed abroad in our hearts, not because he loves us, but because he makes us his lovers: just as the justice of God (Justitia Dei) is that by which we are made just by his gift (justi ejus munere efficimur): and 'salvation of the Lord' by which he saves us: and 'faith of Jesus Christ' that which makes us believers (fideles)."

The words are glossed by the Master of the Sentences, "And this is called the Justice of God, not with which he is just, but because with it he makes us just." At any rate, it seems clear that although in 1509 Luther had not read Augustine's "Spirit and the Letter," he had read an extract concerning this interpretation of the "Justitia Dei" during his study of Peter Lombard.

Denifle's *tour de force* was impressive, and like most polemics of this kind, got a good start of its pursuers. Among many replies the most notable were the essays by Karl Holl and Emmanuel Hirsch.

In the first place, it was pointed out that Luther in speaking of the "use and consent of all doctors" was referring not to Rom. 1:17, but to the "unicum vocabulum" of "Justitia Dei." The distinction is important, for, if granted, it means that the doctors in question were not the exegetes but the systematic theologians, and their views are to be found, not in the commentaries on the Epistles of St. Paul, but in those passages which concerned the conception of divine justice in Commentaries on the Sentences, and the like. Denifle's enormous collection of documents attested a wrong indictment.

Denifle, it is true, could appeal to a passage in Luther's lectures on Genesis, in which he referred to "hunc locum," i.e., Rom. 1:17, as the centre of his difficulties. But these lectures were not published until after Luther's death, and then only in the form in which they were reported. If there is glossing to be done, the 1545 fragment is primary, and Denifle, in his argument, showed some embarrassment at this point. As Holl was not slow to point out, nobody could say how many of Denifle's sixty doctors of the West could have been known, at first- or second-hand, to Luther, or whether he had studied the exegesis concerning Rom. 1:17. Holl proceeded thoroughly to analyse Denifle's authorities and disentangled two main streams of mediaeval exegesis, going back to Ambrosiaster and to Augustine. He showed that Ambrosiaster keeps in mind the problem of the Divine integrity, how the just God can receive sinners, and that while stressing the merciful promises of God, he keeps also the conception of retributive justice. Augustine is less concerned with justice as a divine property than with that bestowed righteousness, the work of grace infused within the human soul, on the ground of which sinners are made just in the presence of God. But Holl pointed out that neither of these expositions, nor all the permutations and combinations of them made thereafter, really met Luther's problem. "That from the time of St. Augustine the Western Church spoke of justifying grace, and that the later schoolmen strengthened this conception by their teaching about an 'habitus' is something known to all, and it is quite certain that Luther was not unaware of it." Emmanuel Hirsch dealt with a notable and fundamental omission from Denifle's authorities, namely, the Nominalist doctors whom Luther knew, and whom he had in mind when he said, "I was taught." He showed that Gabriel Biel, though admitting, even stressing the need for grace, and for the divine "Misericordia," normally preferred to reserve "Justitia" for the retributive justice of God which punishes sinners. This interpretation, which Hirsch based on Biel's commentary on the Sentences, seems confirmed by an examination of some scores of sermons by Biel upon the feasts of the Christian year.

Even more important than these arguments is the abundant testimony of Luther's good faith in this matter which is yielded by writings of other years, many of which, since they had never been published, might well have been completely forgotten by Luther. It is quite certain that, whatever the truth about his statement, it was no later invention, made up at the end of his life. Thus, in 1515:

"Wherefore, if I may speak personally, the word 'Justitia' so nauseated me to hear, that I would hardly have been sorry if somebody had made away with me."

In 1531 (published 1538):

"For thus the Holy Fathers who wrote about the Psalms were wont to expound the 'justus deus' as that in which he vindicates and punishes, not as that which justifies. So it happened to me as a young man, and even today I am as though terrified when I hear God called 'the just.'

"Justice, i.e. grace. This word I learned with much sweat. They used to expound justice as the truth of God which punishes the damned, mercy as that which saves believers. A dangerous opinion which arouses a secret hatred of the heart against God, so that it is terrified when he is so much as named. Justice is that which the Father does when he favours us, with which he justifies, or the gift with which he takes away our sin."

There are three passages in the Table Talk which must embody some core of truth. These suggest that Luther met his difficulty, before he came to the Epistle to the Romans, and in the interpretation of Psalm 31:1. "In justitia tua libera me." But the difficulty, "Justitia Dei" understood as retributive justice, is the same.

Two facts seem clear. First, that in his early career Luther found the conception of the "Justitia Dei" a stumbling block. Second, that this rock of offence did become for him the very corner-stone of his theology. The doctrine of Justification by Faith came to hold, in consequence, for him and for subsequent Protestant theology an altogether more important place than in the Catholic and mediaeval framework. In the sixteenth century men like Sir Thomas More and Stephen Gardiner found it hard to understand what all the Protestant fuss was about, and some striking parallels might be cited among modern Anglican scholars. Thus, even if we had not Luther's explicit testimony in the fragment under consideration, it would be necessary to invent something very like it to account for the remarkable and fundamental transformation in his thought. Denifle's demonstration may be held to have failed in so far as he attempted to show that Luther had wittingly perverted mediaeval teaching, and to have failed, too, in the more fundamental charge that Luther had in fact made no theological discoveries at all.

Thus in his narrative Luther explains simply and clearly why Rom. 1:17 was the climax of his difficulties. Luther already knew and believed that God condemned sinners through the Law. Now, in Rom. 1:17, he found that through the Gospel also was revealed the "Justitia Dei," which he took to mean the strict, retributive justice of God.

If the reader, having absorbed the academic roughage of this critical discussion, will turn back to the autobiographical fragment, he will find it tolerably plain. We can understand how, in the presence of a God who weighted everything against the sinner, Luther was filled with that "huge murmuring" which he elsewhere often and eloquently described, but which a man dared hardly admit to himself, so closely did it approximate to "open blasphemy." This inward ferment added to the outward practices of devotion and penitence an element of strain and unreality, and enforced hypocrisy which in turn aggravated the spiritual conflict. This was not merely an academic affair, though we need not shrink from admitting the theological enquiry of a theological professor into such a category. What he learned and taught about the Justice of God became for him a "carnifex theologistria," however, by reason of the unquiet conscience within. It was this fifth column, within the citadel of the soul, which betrayed him. Miegge's judgment is valid: "In the case of Luther, the religious crisis and the theological crisis are not to be separated."

Henri Daniel-Rops is a member of the French Academy and has written a number of popular works on the history of the church. The following selection gives a view of Luther's evolution toward heresy from a Catholic vantage point.

FROM *The Protestant Reformation* BY *Henri Daniel-Rops*

THE AFFAIR OF THE INDULGENCES

IT WAS 31ST OCTOBER 1517. In the little town of Wittenberg, a part of the Elector of Saxony's possessions, the crush and animation were at their height. Every year the Feast of All Saints attracted countless pious folk, who came to see the precious relics which His Highness the Elector, Frederick the Wise, had collected at great expense, and which were brought out for the occasion from the storerooms of the Schlosskirche. There were plenty of them—several thousand—and they were of the most varied kind: they included not only the complete corpses of various saints, nails from the Passion and rods from the Flagellation, but part of the Child Jesus' swaddling-clothes and some wood from His crib, and even a few drops of His Blessed Mother's milk! Large numbers of most valuable indulgences were attached to the veneration of these distinguished treasures.

That same morning a manifesto, written in scholastic Latin and consisting of ninety-five theses, was found nailed to the door of the castle's chapel. Its author was an Augustinian monk who was extremely well known in the town, and he declared his intention of defending its contents against any opponent prepared to stand up and argue with him. In fact, the document concerned those very indulgences which honest folk were even then showing such eagerness to obtain by praying before the relics and slipping their guilders into the offertory boxes. The pilgrims assembled outside the church heard the more knowledgeable among them translate its words: "Those preaching in favour of indulgences err when they say such indulgences can deliver man and grant him salvation. The man who gives to the poor performs a better action than the one who buys indulgences." There were three hundred yet more bitter lines in this strain. And the worthy pilgrims wondered what could be the purpose of this monk in thus shaking one of the pillars of the Church.

For this was what indulgences seemed to have become: a pillar of the faith. Palz, Master of Erfurt, actually taught that they were "the modern way of preaching the Gospel." Was there anything intrinsically reprehensible about them? A rereading of the treatise which the learned Johann Pfeffer had devoted to the subject a quarter of a century earlier, in that same town of Wittenberg, or a glance at the sermons of the celebrated Johann Geiler of Kayserberg, makes the real meaning of indulgences clear beyond any shadow of a doubt. What the Church understood by *indulgence* was the total or partial remission of the penalties of sin—to which everyone was liable, either on earth or in Purgatory—after the Sacrament of Penance had afforded him absolution from his fault and remission of eternal punishment. But the state of grace was indispensable for the obtaining of such temporal remission; good works, in the shape of prayers, fasting, pilgrimages, visits to churches and almsgiving, were only an incidental, or, to put it another way, a contributory factor. Where there was no firm resolve or inward glow there was no remission. In strict doctrine an indulgence was certainly not an automatic means of gaining a cheap discharge from penalties that were justly deserved. In 1476 a bull of Sixtus IV had recognized that indulgences could be applied to the souls of the departed, whose sufferings in the next world would be alleviated thereby; and the declaration of this principle had contributed to the success of the jubilee of 1500.

It was not of recent origin. As early as the eleventh century crusaders had reaped the benefits of the plenary indulgence. Since then it had been awarded more generally and bestowed on less heroic occasions. It had had a number of happy results, and countless works of religious or social utility had been financed by the money collected in this way; churches too, hospitals, pawnshops, even dikes and bridges. Thanks to indulgences the Church in France had been materially restored on the morrow of the Hundred Years War. Nor had the spiritual results been insignificant: when proclaimed by special preachers the grant of an indulgence provided a spiritual jolt rather like the "missions" of modern times, and was the means of bringing numerous penitents to the confessional.

But it was not these excellent reasons alone which caused the institution to become so widespread, particularly from the fourteenth century onwards. For close on two centuries years of indulgence had been granted with unrestrained liberality in return for the briefest visit to a church, or the least meritorious of pilgrimages. In a period of twelve months the pious Elector Frederick the Wise laid up no fewer than 127,799 years, sufficient to empty a whole province of Purgatory and ensure himself more than one heaven. It is not difficult to imagine the kind of excesses which found their way into this practice, and they had already been condemned in 1312 by the decretal *Abusionibus*. Simony discovered some splendid material here and it is open to doubt whether preachers of indulgences, with their attendant collectors stationed at the foot of the pulpit, where primarily interested in saving souls or in collecting ducats. All too often the grant of an indulgence was part and parcel of some shady deal, and sometimes the right to collect for it was actually sold at auction. Pope Leo X himself once empowered the Fuggers, a celebrated firm of bankers at Augsburg, to preach an indulgence by way of security for a loan. The climate of the age was only too favourable to this type of proceedings. In 1514, when the Hohenzollern Albert of Brandenberg secured his election as Archbishop of Mainz, the heavy chancellery dues of 14,000 ducats, plus a "voluntary settlement" of a further 10,000 intended to ease the scruples of the Curia, were financed by the Fuggers, who were guaranteed in return one-third of the revenues from the great papal indulgence.

Misconduct such as this was not the only menace to the institution; the doctrine itself was affected by something even worse. Far too many preachers taught that an indulgence possessed a kind of magical quality, and that by spending money to obtain it men were taking out a mortgage on Heaven. One popular jingle ran:

Sobald das Geld im Kasten klingt
Die Seele aus dem Fegfeuer springt!

*[As soon as the money in the collection box rings
The soul from out of hellfire springs—Ed.]*

Moreover Germany was not the only country where such rubbish was taught. In 1482 the Sorbonne had condemned one preacher who recited it from the pulpit; at Besançon, in 1486, a certain Franciscan swore that provided a man wore the habit of his Order, St. Francis would come in person to collect him from Purgatory. Naturally enough there were lively reactions to these specious claims. As early as 1484 a priest named Lallier had publicly rejected the view that the Pope had the power to remit the pains of another world by means of indulgence, and despite objections from the theological faculty, the Bishop of Paris had absolved him. In 1498 the Franciscan Vitrier had been hauled before the Sorbonne for having declared that "money must not be given in order to obtain forgiveness." His disciple Erasmus had lately written: "Any trader, mercenary soldier or judge has but to put down his money, however nefariously acquired, and he imagines that he has purged the whole Lemean Marsh of his life." Views of this sort were taught in the University of Wittenberg, which considered itself the rival of Leipzig and Erfurt; and trenchancy of tone helped to further the renown of that centre, where, during 1516, statements such as the following had been heard: "It is an absurdity to preach that the souls in Purgatory are ransomed by indulgences."

In 1517 the most important indulgence preached in Germany was that which the popes had twice accorded to generous Christians donating money for the new basilica of St. Peter's: Julius II in 1506, in order that building might begin, and Leo X in 1514, to enable it to continue. It was the fruits of this indulgence which had been the object of that extraordinary share-out which we have already noticed on the occasion of the Mainz election. The archbishop had entrusted the task of preaching the indulgence to the Dominicans, and this had provoked a fraternal but somewhat bitter jealousy among the Augustinians.

At the head of these preachers was a certain Brother Tetzel, a burly, voluble fellow, who pleaded his case with extreme enthusiasm. He was a well-intentioned man, whose own moral conduct was perfectly honourable, and he did not deserve the calumnies with which his opponents were to befoul him; but his theology was highly questionable. His method of procedure merely increased the public belief that an indulgence was a mere financial transaction. He visited the whole area dependent on Mainz, and would arrive with a vast retinue, preceded by the bull which was carried on a velvet cushion embroidered with gold. The people would come out in procession to meet him, accompanied by the ringing of bells and waving of banners; and Tetzel would then mount the pulpit, or stand in the town square, offering "passports to cross the sea of wrath and go direct to Paradise." This was indeed a splendid opportunity to make certain of escaping the seven years of suffering—which, as all agreed, any forgiven sin still required in the Beyond—by obtaining the plenary indulgence accorded by a confessor of Tetzel's choice. Besides, here also was an opportunity to snatch some friend or loved one from the fires of Purgatory. Nor was the price extortionate. The penitent must go to confession, visit seven churches, recite five *Paters* and five *Aves*, and place an offering in the indulgence box. The offering demanded was a modest one, scaled to the resources of each individual believer: for the poorest a quarter of a florin was sufficient.

It was against such practices and such teaching that the manifesto nailed to the door of the Schlosskirche protested so strongly. Tetzel had not preached in Wittenberg, which was Saxon territory, but all recognized the target of this attack. It was all very well for the author to maintain discretion by advising his readers to receive "the Apostolic Commissioners with respect"; his theses rejected not only the Dominican's interpretation of the indulgence, but protested against the institution itself. He denounced its financial side. "The indulgences so extolled by preachers have only one merit, that of bringing in money." Or again: "Nowadays the Pope's money-bag is fatter than those of the richest capitalists; why does he not build this basilica with his own resources rather than with the offerings of the poor?" These somewhat clumsy arguments made a deep impression among the common people. He also criticized the theological bases of the institution, suggesting that the indulgences caused men to lose their sense of penitence. "True contrition gladly accepts the penalties and seeks them out; indulgence remits them and inspires us with aversion for them. When a Christian is truly penitent he has the right to plenary remission, even without an ecclesiastical indulgence. The grace of Jesus Christ remits the penalties of sin, not the Pope. Man can hope to receive this grace by experiencing a hatred of self and of his sin, and not by the accomplishment of a few acts or the sacrifice of a little money." Although, in so far as they contain authentic Catholic doctrine, these theses are acceptable in many respects, they deviate from orthodoxy to the extent that they deny the Pope's power to remit penalties and refer implicitly to a theory of grace according to which man's merits are almost worthless.

What motive had impelled the author of this document to defy the official teaching of the Church? Indignation against traffickers in sacred things? Undoubtedly. Hatred of the Pope and contempt for the simoniacal Roman Curia? No. There was something deeper, more decisive, and it is revealed in the very last sentence of his ninety-five theses. Tetzel was trying to persuade the faithful that salvation was easily effected through works; he was concealing from his hapless listeners that it is necessary "to enter Heaven by way of many tribulations," as the Acts of the Apostles makes quite clear; he was encouraging them to "rest in false security." Here was the crux of the matter. It was against "this appalling error" that the professor of Wittenberg entered the lists; and he entered them with all the violence of a man for whom this theological dispute represented a drama played out in his own life, and whom false security had brought very close indeed to total despair and unbelief. His name was *Martin Luther*.

A BRILLIANT YOUNG MONK

At this date Luther was a tall, bony man with powerful expressive hands. They were never still: they were forever pointing at an enemy or punctuating an argument. Everything about him indicated a passion, unease and a latent violence that was always on the verge of erupting to produce total destruction. The eyes in the rough-hewn face, with its high cheekbones, square chin and lined cheeks, often sparkled with anger or intelligence, but no less frequently they allowed a glimpse of uncontrollable anguish. It is difficult to escape the fascination which this monk in his simple Augustinian robe exerted on everyone who saw him. In 1517 he was thirty-four years old.

What had Luther's life been like up to this time? What events and reasoning had led him to quarrel openly with official conformity and make the gesture which, by setting him in the forefront of world affairs, was to turn him into the living symbol of contradiction? The *Rückblick*, that rapid and superficial glance which he threw back to his youth in 1545, a year before his death, is hardly an adequate answer to these questions; when old people evoke their memories they very often amend both truth and falsehood.

As for the traditional account, still widely believed, it seems best to retain here only the bare outline of the facts and not their substance. The explanation of Martin Luther's attitude must not be sought in his allegedly unhappy childhood and adolescence, nor, as the psychoanalysts would have it, in the crisis of a monk beset by temptations of the flesh, nor even in the scandalized indignation he is supposed to have felt during a brief visit to Rome. It is to be found rather in an inner conflict, something like those experienced by St Paul, St Augustine and Pascal—a conflict through which Luther lived in keen spiritual agony and uncertainty, and from which he unhappily emerged along a path which was no longer that approved by Mother Church.

Martin Luther was born on 10th November 1483, at Eisleben in Saxony, the second of eight children. He was brought up at Mansfeld, where Hans, his father, had settled six months after the boy's birth. His early years were no more and no less happy than that of many sons of ordinary folk. The harsh realities of life brutalized this class of persons, and in a large family there was no time for emotional refinement. Hans was a devout, stern man whose morals were irreproachable but who was easily roused to anger. He was striving with all his might to rise from artisan to foreman, and finally to become a small foundry owner on his own account, and his sole desire was that his entire household should behave with absolute propriety. Hans Luther's hardworking wife, Margaret, *née* Ziegler, was a stolid Franconian. She did not find it difficult to share her husband's ideas and she directed her family with a firm hand which her children occasionally found too heavy.

Martin's parents sent him to school at Mansfeld when he was six years old. There he received the customary education of the age, consisting of the old *trivium* and the catechism, instilled by the pedagogic methods which were then in current use and in which the cane played a large part. When it became apparent that he was an exceptionally gifted boy, his father decided that he should continue his studies with a view to the law. He spent a year in the Cathedral School at Magdeburg, which was excellently conducted by the Brethren of the Common Life, and there he acquired an unhappily all too brief experience of genuine spirituality: it was most probably here that he made his first real contact with the Bible. Then, because his great-uncle was sacristan of St Nicholas's, Luther was drawn back to Eisenach, and there he developed his innate talents for music. Finally, at the age of eighteen, he entered Erfurt University—his father, who was now more comfortably off, was henceforth able to pay him an allowance—where he obtained an outstanding degree and greatly improved his powers of self-expression and reasoning. His teachers, Fathers Usingen and Palz, trained him in their methods, which were those of Ockhamist scholasticism. His fellow students regarded him as an honourable, devout, but merry companion. So far everything about Luther's life had been utterly normal and ordinary. Then, just as he had begun his legal studies, an unforeseen event completely altered his destiny.

On 2nd July 1505, while he was returning alone from Mansfeld to Erfurt, a thunderstorm of unusual violence suddenly broke upon him. The lightning flashed so close that he believed himself lost. In the midst of this danger he invoked St Anne according to custom, and promised: "If you come to my aid I will become a monk." This was perhaps a rash vow, but it was certainly not spontaneous. Various other incidents had preceded this spiritual decision. Legend has embroidered upon them so much that their detail has become obscured, but their meaning is abundantly plain. A serious illness during adolescence, the sudden death of a friend, a sword wound acquired in a student's duel and which had bled for a long time—all these had brought Luther face to face with the one great fact that youth tends to ignore— the fact of death. The episode of the thunderstorm set the seal on this revelation. Luther's impressionable nature and naturally vivid sensibility responded urgently to that mortal fear which the thunderclap had inspired in his soul. He remembered the good Brethren of the Common Life, the Anhalt ruler in the Franciscan habit whom he had known at Magdeburg, and dedicated young Carthusians he often saw at Erfurt. He thought of all the people he knew who seemed to have found peace of heart, and the answer to the most dreadful of all questions beneath the homespun of the monastic robe. This vow of his was undoubtedly forced from his soul by terror, but the terror was not caused by the thunderstorm alone. Neither his family nor his friends could prevent him from remaining faithful to his promise. Fifteen days after the incident on the Erfurt road he set off to knock on the door of the Augustinian monastery there.

In 1517 then, when he nailed his theses on the door of the Schlosskirche in Wittenberg, he was a monk—and a monk of some importance in his Order—and he was moreover a monk who had not the slightest desire to renounce his vows. "I have been a pious monk for twenty years," he was to say; "I have said a Mass every day; I have worn myself out in prayer and fasting." Witnesses have described him as a good monk, "certainly not without sin, but above serious reproach." In 1507 he was ordained priest. Luther mounted the altar steps for the first time with an ardour mingled with fear, as befitted one who was about to hold the living God in his own hands. Theology had made him increasingly fervent; Duns Scotus and St Thomas, Pierre d'Ailly and Gerson, William of Ockham and others in the same tradition, notable Gabriel Biel, had been the object of his voracious reading, together with the Bible, and St Augustine, and all the mystics from St Bernard to Master Eckhart. In 1508, by order of Staupitz, the wise Vicar-General for Germany, who was much interested in this brilliant young man, Luther was transferred to Wittenberg, there to teach philosophy and acquire the title of Bachelor of Arts. He enjoyed a high reputation in his Order.

This was made very clear when, during the winter of 1510–11, he was chosen to go to Rome to submit the dispute between the Augustinians of the strict and conventual observances to the superiors of the Order. Legend has it that what he saw in the Eternal City so upset the young monk that he resolved to undertake the reform of the Church. This is a convenient story, but all the evidence is against it. Luther stayed in Rome for four short weeks, behaving like any other pious pilgrim. He was most anxious to see as many churches as possible, to win the indulgences attached to these visits and to climb the "scala sancta" on his knees; in short, as he himself recalled, he was filled with "holy madness." All he saw of the Papal Court were the usual glimpses that any humble visiting German cleric might expect to obtain. He obviously heard a good deal of gossip, but this did not have much immediate effect upon him. It was not until much later on, when he had been condemned by the Catholic Church, that he sought to justify his own attitude by reviving his memories of Rome. So great was men's ignorance in the capital of Christendom, he recalled, that he had been unable to find a confessor there; in St Sebastian's he had seen seven priests hurry through the Mass within the hour at a single altar; and he himself had witnessed the shameless behaviour of women in church. Perhaps; but he did not pronounce these strictures until twenty-five years after the incidents concerned—very much *a posteriori*.

On his return to Germany Luther was assigned to the Augustinian house in Wittenberg; in the following year, having been made doctor of theology, he was awarded the chair of Holy Scripture at the university. His lectures were outstandingly successful: he spoke on the Psalms and the Pauline Epistles; he was also a celebrated preacher, highly regarded by his congregations. Staupitz, his immediate superior, had a very exalted opinion of him; he made him "district vicar," in other words, provincial, with jurisdiction over eleven of the Order's houses; and he even went so far as to tell Luther: "God speaks through your mouth." Thus Luther's importance and prestige added considerable weight to his stand against the preachers of indulgences on All Saints' Eve 1517.

The Drama of a Soul

In order to understand Luther's reasons for acting as he did we must penetrate his soul and reach into those dark and dangerous recesses of the mind wherein each man worthy of the name seeks, amid suffering and contradiction, to give a meaning to his own destiny. Because the light which he himself sheds upon the drama of his youth was given long after the period concerned, a number of critics have treated it all as legend. The aged Luther, they allege, invented the background of a Pascalian debate in order to provide his rebellion with fundamentally lofty and mystical origins. But an impartial study of the documents covering the decisive years—for example, his commentary on the Epistle to the Romans—is sufficient to convince the reader that their author could have adopted certain attitudes at the end of a secret and painful effort to find the answer to the gravest of man's problems.

Anyone who refuses to believe that Luther was fundamentally one of those individuals for whom life and belief are serious matters is guilty of traducing historical and psychological truth. He was essentially a protagonist in great spiritual battles. The Augustinian monk who seemed to be making for himself such a brilliant career was inwardly tormented by that peculiarly religious anxiety which it is easier to feel than to define.

Luther had entered the monastery hoping to discover peace of mind, but he had not found it. He was very much a son of his age and of his native land—of Germany, where man's struggle against the powers of darkness was translated into a multitude of terrible or sublime legends; of Christianity at the crossroads, where morbid sermons and dances of death caused the faithful to be haunted with thoughts of their ultimate destiny. He had not been able to get rid of these phantoms merely by donning the monastic robe. "I know a man," he wrote in 1518, "who declared he has experienced such mortal terror that no words can describe it; he who has not suffered the like would never believe him. But it is a fact that if anyone were obliged to endure for long, for half an hour or even the tenth part of an hour, he would perish utterly, and his very bones would be reduced to ashes." Luther was in the grip of terrible anguish, and his friend Melanchthon relates that during the whole of his monastic life he was never able to throw it off. "My heart bled when I said the Canon of the Mass," Luther confesses, in reference to his years as a young priest. These are words that no one can read without emotion.

Whence came this anguish? Certain authors have suggested that it was caused by hereditary neurosis, but there is no real proof of this. It is perfectly clear to anyone reading many of his own confessions that Luther was not so much a sick man as one burdened with the tragic sense of sin in all its intensity. But of what sin? It is futile to pretend to find an answer in the stirrings of his flesh. Some have seen Luther as a monk in the grip of secret lusts, a familiar of the *delectatio morosa*, unable to quell the beast within him and revolting against the discipline of the Church in order to satisfy his craving. Yet if this were a true picture, if he had acted on the strength of such contemptible motives, his influence would scarcely have been so far-reaching, and would scarcely have inflicted so much suffering upon the Church. Besides, Luther himself frequently emphasized that the worst temptations were not carnal: "evil thoughts, hatred of God, blasphemy, despair and unbelief—these are the main temptations." The concupiscence which he had to conquer was not primarily that which draws male to female, but an irresistible craving of both body and soul that urges man to embrace all that is terrestrial and manifest—in a word, human—deflecting him from the invisible and divine.

In the monastery he had hoped to be delivered from these monsters. He was a mystical personality in many ways, and he dreamed of a warm, consoling presence which would shield him from evil and from himself, but he had discovered nothing in the monastic routine to provide such comfort. Was this because he lacked true humility, or because he had not the spirit of prayer? Only God, who has already judged the soul of Martin Luther, can supply an answer. One obstacle, however, certainly prevented him from running like the Prodigal Son to the arms of his Father, for whenever the least flicker of impurity, violence or doubt crossed his mind he believed himself damned. He tried prayer, asceticism, and even daily confession, but none of them could rid him of this ever-present obsession with hell, which continually threatened to overwhelm him. "I did penance," Luther says, "but despair did not leave me."

The obstacle which barred Luther's way to the path of peace and love was his concept of God. He insists that this was the picture shown him in religious life. "We paled at the mere mention of Christ's Name, for He was always depicted as a stern judge who was angry with us." Was it necessary to work oneself to death in prayer, fasting and mortifications from fear of a Master wielding the rod of chastisement, a Divine Executioner? What was the good of it all, since one could not even be sure of melting His wrath? "When will you do enough to obtain God's mercy?" he asked himself in anguish. In that age of misery the message of Christ's love seemed sterile; there remained only the atrocious doctrine of inevitable punishment meted out by an inexorable judge.

It has not been difficult for Catholic critics to show that this doctrine has never been that of Holy Church. In a book of no fewer than 378 pages, Father Denifle has conclusively demonstrated that the "justice of God" mentioned in a famous passage of the Epistle to the Romans (1:17), and which Luther took to be the supreme spiritual reality, was intended to signify something far more than *justitia puniens*, divine wrath punishing the sins of men; the words were used rather of sanctifying grace, of the omnipotent mercy lavished by God on all who believe in Him and submit to His ordinances. Luther's interpretation of the phrase reveals a surprising failure to understand the philosophy of such writers as St Augustine and St Bernard, with whose works he was undoubtedly well acquainted. To explain the spiritual drama of the young Augustinian monk, however, it is sufficient to acknowledge that he himself regarded this erroneous doctrine as valid, and as that which his own professors had taught him.

The fact may have been due to the imperfect theological training offered by the representations of decadent scholasticism who filled all the university chairs. Moreover the teaching then in fashion contained one feature calculated to impel a restless soul along the downward slope. To such a man as Luther, obsessed with the desire to appease his terrible God, and deriving not the slightest comfort from his prayers and mortifications, one system in particular provided a kind of answer: Ockhamist Nominalism, in which, as we have seen, he had been brought up. Luther had discovered from the writings of this school not only that man could overcome sin by will alone, but also that no human action became meritorious unless God acknowledged it and willed it to be so. But if man's will failed it had no means of recovery, for reason was unavailing and grace was not conceived as a supernatural principle raising man's spiritual forces to the level of Divine Justice. Thus nothing was left save a capricious God, granting or withholding His grace and forgiveness for motives that defied all the rules of logic. Before Him stood a defenceless man, inert and passive in relation to the work of salvation. Destiny appeared to be regulated by the cold mechanics of a despot in whose eyes nothing had any merit. Luther strove hard to find confirmation of these theories in certain passages of St Paul and St Augustine, for they corresponded all too well with his fundamental and powerful belief in the futility of all human effort. In several respects he remained an Ockhamist all his life; but he rejected the voluntarism taught by Ockham's disciples, he denied the human liberty which they recognized, and he gave it a ring of predestination-ism which was absent from the master's philosophy. None of this did anything to grant him peace of mind.

But a number of more peaceful influences were at work. Luther had read all the mystics, especially the German writers of the late Middle Ages, notably Tauler. Here too he had found elements that tended to deny the importance of external works, to discard free will and to exalt the part played by faith in Christ the Redeemer. Man must lay himself open to God's action, submit to it and do nothing to resist it. This was one of the fundamental ideas of the *Theologica Germanica.* Furthermore Staupitz, anxious to heal this ravaged soul, had gone a long way in the same direction by showing Luther the gentleness of God's love and the need for supreme surrender to Providence. Neither the subtleties of the schools more ritual practices would give him the divine life to which he aspired, but only the impulse of a believing soul, and the piety which sprang from the most secret recesses of the heart. "True repentance begins with love of justice and of God." Once the young monk felt that part of his burden had been lifted, that he was on the way to a new enlightenment; and it seemed that ideas, arguments and biblical references poured in from all sides to confirm this doctrine "and dance a jig around it."

It was now that there happened the "discovery of mercy," a wholly spiritual event to which Luther's disciples afterwards traced the origins of the Reformation. The date and place of this occurrence are the subject of some dispute. He may have had his first glimpse of it in Rome, while making the pious pilgrimage on his knees up the "Scala sancta." It may, on the other hand, be necessary to advance the date to 1518 or 1519; if so he can have had only a kind of presentiment of his doctrine on the day when he nailed his theses to the chapel door. Its main features, however, are already apparent in the university lectures which he gave between 1514 and 1517. The most probable truth is that the "discovery" took place in his mind by gradual stages, before imposing itself on his soul with such force that all arguments and reservations became as nothing in the blinding clarity of what seemed to him to be incontrovertible evidence.

In the preface to the 1545 edition of his *Works* Luther describes in detail this "sudden illumination of the Holy Spirit." He was pondering once again the terrible seventeenth verse in the first chapter of the Epistle to the Romans when the true meaning—that is to say, the meaning he henceforth considered to be true—was revealed to him. "While I pursued my meditations day and night, examining the import of these words, 'The justice of God is revealed in the Gospel, as it is written, the just live by faith,' I began to understand that the justice of God signifies that justice whereby the just live through the gift of God, namely, through faith. Therefore the meaning of the sentence is as follows: "the Gospel shows us the justice of God, but it is a passive justice, through which, by means of faith, the God of mercy justifies us." To the young monk, tortured by fear and anguish, this was indeed a prodigious discovery! The hangman God, armed with His whip, faded away, yielding place to Him towards whom the soul could turn with perfect trust and confidence. . . .

At this juncture, as always happens where great minds are concerned, all kinds of reflections and arguments crystallized around this one apparently quite straightforward idea. It became the basis of a system. "System" is perhaps the wrong word here; for Luther there was no question of dry doctrine or paper thesis, but of a vital experience, the answer to all his own terrible problems. But he saw the answer so clearly that he was able to express it in the form of categorical principles. Man is a sinner, incapable of making himself just (i.e. righteous) and condemned to impotence by the enemy he bears within himself. Even though he conforms outwardly to the law, he remains in a state of sin. Even though he tries to behave righteously and hopes to acquire merit, he is unable to do so, for at the root of his very being there is a deadly germ. There must therefore be, and indeed there is, a justice exterior to man, which alone will save him. Through the grace of Jesus Christ all the soul's blemishes are, as it were, covered by a cloak of light. Thus the one means and only hope of salvation is to entrust oneself to Christ, as it were, to cling to Him. "The faith that justifies is that which seizes Jesus Christ." Compared with this saving reality all man's miserable efforts towards repentance and self-improvement were ridiculous and worthless. "The just live by faith."

It must be admitted that this view was perfectly adapted to set an anguished soul at rest. Where did it deviate from the orthodox? The Church teaches that God is "just" in the simplest sense of the term, that is to say, He distributes His graces to us all in an equitable manner, and not by virtue of a kind of incomprehensible caprice. She teaches that salvation and eternal bliss are earned in the world through positive effort and good works. She affirms the importance of sin, but she refuses to admit that man can do nothing to combat it. She does indeed proclaim the indispensability of the love of God and union with Christ, but she asserts that they demand from man a positive effort to acquire a supernatural resemblance. Faith is but the beginning of justification. It is completed by reception of the sacrament, in the act of contribution or the act of charity. Salvation demands much more than mere belief.

Luther, however, was so intoxicated by his discovery, so exalted by the joy of escaping at last from the vice which had held him in its grip, that he would consider no argument advanced against his theory. "I felt suddenly born anew," he said, "and it seemed that the doors of Paradise itself were flung wide open to me, and I entered in." He was saved! He knew he was a sinner, but Christ had taken upon His shoulders the sins of the whole world. It was distasteful to realize that all the pious exercises and all the theological reasoning to which he had recourse were of no effect, but in the blinding light of the Redemption all human things were nothing but dry dust. The dialectic of sin and grace contained the answer to everything. The exultant professor of Wittenberg announced his discovery at all his lectures even before his own philosophy had been fully defined, before it had been crowned with the maxim (not formulated until after 1518) that in order to be saved all that one needed was the inner certainty of one's own salvation. He set out his thesis at Easter 1517, at the beginning of a series of lectures on the Epistle to the Hebrews. "Man is incapable of obtaining relief from any sin by his own efforts alone. In the sight of God all human virtues are sin." He also directed one of his pupils, Bernhardi, to take "Grace and Free Will" as the subject of his thesis for the doctorate; it was to conform in all respects with the principles of Luther, who later admitted that at this period he felt "divinely possessed."

The preaching of indulgences offered Luther a splendid opportunity to make the truth blindingly clear to everyone. He was disgusted most of all by this computation of so-called merits shamefully acquired, in order to escape the just pains of the after-life. He himself enjoyed true security in that prodigious wager upon Christ which he intended to maintain from now onwards. The false, pitiable thing which these wretched folk believed that they acquired, by kneeling in front of some relics and throwing their money into a box provided by someone like Tetzel, was no true security. As for the authority of the Pope, who guaranteed the value of such practices, the Ockhamist in Luther recalled what the leaders of that school had had to say, their reservations on papal infallibility and indeed on the function of the Papacy in general. He remembered Gabriel Biel's declaration that every Catholic was competent to reform the Church. He had, of course, not the slightest idea that in adopting positions of this kind he was going to set in motion the gravest crisis which Christianity had ever experienced. He was, in his own words, "a blind wretch who set off without knowing where he was going." Spiritual argument did not really interest him. He was fundamentally interested only in making the world hear and understand Heaven's response to his *De Profundis*; but "the voice of Germany, restless and secretly trembling with unrestrained passion," was not slow to answer his cry, and the drama of one soul unleashed a revolution.